REDEFINING CORPORATE SPECTRUM

THE SECRET TO CHANGING AND UPHOLDING DIVERSITY, INCLUSION, BELONGING, AND EQUALITY IN ORGANISATIONS.

DR. AMIT DAS

To

All my bosses and mentors who made a difference in my professional career.

"Even the most progressive businesses are still developing their understanding of how to lessen hiring prejudice, promote inclusion, and generate a sense of belonging for employees from all backgrounds. Making your organisation more diverse will force your team members to examine their prejudices and presumptions."

– Dr. Amit Das, Motivational Speaker, Leadership Coach , Counsellor, and Mentor.

Contents

Foreword

"If you believe, as we believe, that diversity leads to better products, and we're all about making products that enrich people's lives, then you obviously put a ton of energy behind diversity the same way you would put a ton of energy behind anything else that is truly important." – Tim Cook

Dear Reader,

Thank you for taking your precious time to learn more about " Redefining Corporate Spectrum". This book aims to close the gap between what businesses are saying and doing to advance diversity, inclusion, belonging, and equality (DIBE) what are truly required to bring about real change and foster genuine diversity and inclusion in the workplace.

In this book, the author explains how women contribute significantly to the workplace and how they may realise their full potential by cooperating with others rather than competing with them, which will increase their success, prosperity, and positive outlook on life generally.

"If you want to fulfil the promise of genuine equality, you must stop using expensive, ineffectual tactics and instead focus on changing entrenched racial prejudices."

The workforce of today has shown that both men and women are capable of working well together as a team. Women in the workplace; gender disparity in the office; and the fact that women are not less valuable than men; a woman also has more to give than just her physical beauty; the influence of women in business and the corporate sphere; the advantages of having more women in leadership roles in the workplace; these are all topics covered in this book. The book sharply contrasts the lofty language of diversity, inclusion, belongling, and equality with actual accomplishments.

With tips on how to properly negotiate the workplace, this book serves as a reminder of how valuable women are. It gives men an understanding of the contributions that women make to the workplace and teaches them how to interact with, support, and gain from working with them. It offers insights on how organisations and larger society's structures, procedures, and rules occasionally obstruct women's ability to fully realise the value of their contributions to the workplace, as well as suggestions for how to do so. From the perspective of a vast array of men, perspectives on the value of women contribute to the workplace, highlighting some of the things that women offer to the organisation that are specifically their own. All of this combines to provide a framework that enables the full recognition of women's worth at work and a more equitable and effective working environment for everyone.

You'll discover while reading this book why fostering a sense of community among all employees is the new yardstick for employee engagement. You can become familiar with the major concepts behind DIBE (Diversity, Inclusion, Belonging, and Equality) and why they are important. You may evaluate the current state of your organisation. You can specify and carry out the baby steps required to instil new organisational culture muscle memory. Employee cooperation, innovation, communication, and a sense of belonging may all be improved. You can gain confidence in your ability to overcome DIBE-related problems in the future. You can gain support from coworkers and stakeholders who can clearly see how to move forward and why.

The book examines how communication as an organising phenomenon underlies systemic and institutionalised biases and generates practises that favour some groups while excluding or marginalising others. It does this by connecting communication theories to diversity and inclusion, and making clear that inclusion is about the communication processes of organisations, institutions, and communities.

This book will assist you in implementing organisational development ideas to create culture transformation. It walks you through the essential elements of implementing change at every stage of employee life, as well as in your supply chain and product development. Importantly, it will support you in having a real influence on your organisation through your workforce, both now and in the future. In order to study issues of inclusion and exclusion, which have become a significant concern as both society and the workforce become more diverse, organising inclusion brings together communication specialists.

Organisational stakeholders, human resource professionals, and policy makers, as well as academics and students working in the domains of communication, management, and organisational studies, will find the book of considerable interest.

This book will give a thorough explanation and analysis of diversity and inclusion in the modern economy. Businesses and professionals may use it to discover how they might work together in the future to increase diversity, inclusion, and equality. This book explores ways to create green transitions that respect, benefit, and integrate disadvantaged social groups.

This book examines the difficulty of incorporating problems of fairness and justice into the green revolution and demonstrates how doing so runs the risk of widening the gap between the wealthy and the poor, the excluded and the included.

This book explains how leaders and businesses who embrace and incorporate inclusion and diversity into their organisation can profit with clarity, and the most recent research. These are the companies that will innovate and adapt more quickly. They will have a working culture that attracts and retains the best new talent. They will reach a larger group of clients and consumers that respect and appreciate them. They are aware that leaders and companies must take inclusion and diversity seriously both now and in the future if they are to reap these benefits and many more. The author's three poignant, cutting-edge chapters demonstrate how the time for productive DIBE has come, exactly, and show how to apply inclusive leadership skills; ensure that communication is important and data matters; enhance business values with purposeful action and positive results; celebrate success using incentive and accountability applications; building a productive hybrid workplace; debias systems and ensure inclusive hiring; achieve parity in reviews, retention, and promotion; and build inclusive foundations.

This book is your entryway to superior experience if you want to improve the workplace and, therefore, the planet. This authoritative, but amusing, and well-told tour of the realm of workplace diversity is fascinating and thorough. This is a significant book that serves as an indispensable guide for anybody learning about the value of diversity in today's society. This book is intended for business executives, HR specialists, and anybody with managerial responsibilities.

This book, is comprehensive even though it is brief and easy to read, and it offers effective and approachable advice to a readership that has never needed it more. It is feasible to stop prejudice. This book offers convincing arguments for why it is crucial to pay attention to gender diversity and inclusion in this specific period in our global economy. It takes the guesswork out of what to do next by outlining the value proposition of gender diversity and inclusion in straightforward terms.

Each individual feels accepted for who they are because of belonging. The author provides guidance on how to lead the discussion on DIBEs, recruit and keep a diverse workforce, pay attention to workers, and include DIBEs into your employee life cycle.

Discover how to implement a diversity, inclusion, belonging, and equality (DIBE) programme suited to the particular requirements of your business. In this book, he explains how to ask the right questions and choose the best partners and programme advocates to discover precisely what your business needs. He provides guidance on how to win support for DIBEs from top executives and employees alike, while also seeking out and incorporating participant input.

This book is highly recommended by renowned and knowledgeable professionals who will help you reach your aims of changing your thinking to help the world move past injustice. You gain from this book in a number of ways. If you want to change the world for the better, this book is your key to getting there!

Thank you for taking the time to read this book.

So, happy reading and learning to all my readers.

Carpe diem.

Dr. Amit Das

Motivational Speaker, Leadership Coach, Counsellor, and Mentor.

Preface

"We are building products that people with very diverse backgrounds use, and I think we all want our company makeup to reflect the makeup of the people who use our products." — Sheryl Sandberg

The word "diversity" has gained popularity and is being promoted by prestigious organisations. Industry executives have given hundreds of millions of dollars to start training programmes, engage consultants and diversity, and guarantee that their businesses reflect the racial and cultural mix of the nation. But is it effective?

This book discusses how to enhance the diversity and inclusion of your business by carefully considering the possibilities and problems they provide. Learn how to support a diverse workforce through sensible management, carefully crafted dialogues, and a culture that recognises and values each team member's individual contribution.

Organisations must take a more comprehensive approach to inclusion and diversity if they are to make a significant and lasting change. A departure from engrained traditions, a change in thinking, a redesign of organisational culture, and a change in leadership behaviour are nonetheless necessary for this. Organisations have, with a few exceptions, fallen well short of their objectives despite decades of hand wringing, expensive efforts, and awkward dialogues.

"When you consider diversity, inclusion, belonging, and equality (DIBE), you put the human behind objectives, statistics, processes, compliance, and audits."

A society that celebrates diversity includes people from many racial, ethnic, and cultural origins. Inclusion entails asking various groups to participate in workplace activities. You've undoubtedly heard these phrases before if you pay attention to talks concerning human resources. All that people really desire is to fit in. We must band together because of this. And it's my desire that we may come together in a really genuine way where we celebrate and learn from one another's diversity.

Therefore, a psychologically secure workplace is one in which a climate of mutual respect and trust encourages employees to provide their best efforts at work, be more considerate of their coworkers, and guide the business toward its objectives. Diversity is therefore simply the first step; true value and effect are produced at work via diversity, inclusion, belonging, and equality.

I will discuss topics from several communication, ranging from social and environmental activism to concerns with racism, gender, sexual orientation, age, and ability. In this book, I'll discuss what belonging is, why it matters, and how to create a sense of belonging at work. Organising DIBE is an intellectual resource for enhancing theoretical knowledge and practical applications that come with an ever-greater diversity of individuals cooperating, participating, and working together.

This book takes a position and welcomes the potential that genuine diversity and inclusion provide for any business in any sector. As the author provides tried-and-true methods for enabling individuals in your whole organisation to fully utilise their abilities and potential to influence good organisational change and the future of work, be ready to open your heart and be inspired.

"You grow in knowledge, become more open to everyone, and improve as a group when you listen and enjoy both the similarities and differences."

In terms of how organisations are organised and run on a daily basis, the business world of today is one that is marked by perpetual development, constant advancement, and constant progress. However, there are still a lot of organisations that have enormous gaps in crucial areas of social and interpersonal growth. Gender, colour, ethnicity, age, and background are the main components of diversity, inclusion, belonging, and equality.

"Many organisations today, throughout the world, suffer from a severe lack of diversity and inclusion."

Despite the fact that many organisations are making substantial efforts to diversify their workforces and integrate inclusion and diversity more deeply into their cultures and business models, current advancements do not properly make workplaces diverse or inclusive.

This benchmark book brings coverage of research techniques in DIBE up to date and enhances the field's research, even if present research procedures usually fall short of addressing the issues faced in DIBE research. The book is a priceless contribution to the body of knowledge, especially for DIBE students and researchers working in the areas of marketing and entrepreneurship as well as human resource management, strategic management, and organisation. Diversity and inclusion in the workplace are topics that are being discussed more now than ever before.

In order to go deeper into this, this book will emphasise many aspects of diversity and inclusion, such as their definition in business and the history, evolution, and current growth of these concepts. Additionally, this book will emphasise the typical difficulties, drawbacks, advantages, and best practises of diversity and inclusion. This book will focus on how diversity and inclusion may be enhanced, important business principles, data, and current business model implementation strategies.

This book demonstrates, with the help of real-world examples, how to activate responsibility, make inclusive policies visible, energise your taskforce, implement beneficial incentives and awards, create balanced scorecards, and recognise accomplishments. This extremely relevant book provides examples of the most recent recruiting and team-building processes to guarantee everyone's inclusion, diversity equity, and bias-free systems.

"When people bring their complete, real selves to work, organisations gain from diversity. Teams with more diversity are more creative, inventive, and engaged. Sharing and voicing opinions regarding professional and personal experiences that may change depending on one's identity are examples of being authentic at work."

After reading through each chapter, there are specific activities offered at the conclusion that may be taken to change the world and make a deliberate contribution. The book as a whole offers a simple, interactive playbook that explains how to optimise a business for inclusion and diversity. How to achieve genuine productivity, performance, and profit in a global setting, resulting in true social sustainability for all humanity.

Everybody around us has limitless potential that we have the power to realise. With the help of this book, you may all be in charge of bringing out the best in each other and in strangers, as well as in your coworkers. This book serves as both the key to unlock that potential and the catalyst to get you started.

We all have the capacity to make the world a better place. Through multidisciplinary, comparative, and critical viewpoints, explores the multifaceted nature of equality, diversity, and inclusion in the workplace. Diversity and inclusion are not the newest trends in business. It is much more than the annual wage difference reporting obligations; it is not a simple check box activity. In the end, it's here to stay!

Therefore, let's discuss this book and what it is and isn't. I'm going to assist you in determining where you are beginning from, what you need, how to gain support, and how to maintain momentum once you have achieved success. You'll need to do a more strategic study on DIBEs in order to accomplish your organisation's unique goals when it comes to more focused objectives like hiring and employee retention.

DIBE's overarching objectives are to foster a sense of community and equity within your business. So if you keep coming back, you'll discover in this book where you may learn about subjects like inclusive mentality, cultural humility, and collaborative manpower. In the realm of DIBE's, there is a lot to learn, but it is well worth the effort.

An element or somebody inside your current culture who may assist you in realising your ultimate goal of diversity, inclusion, and equality is a DIBE asset. Individual DIBE advocates and corporate principles that may support your roll out are the resources we're exploring today. Let's examine each of these in more detail.

The workplace has become more inclusive and varied thanks to the efforts of compassionate managers, which has helped to create a genuine sense of security. Their efforts in this area have resulted in increased production and have had a beneficial effect on me personally, making me feel included and at home.

Given the rapidly shifting workforce demographics, high-profile discrimination cases in the news, and the implementation of new laws, it is more important than ever that businesses understand and effectively manage workplace diversity in order to boost business results and foster an inclusive workplace that upholds social responsibility. This book presents an in-depth and contextual overview of enduring and cutting-edge topics and approaches to diversity and inclusion management. It is jam-packed with learning elements to stimulate critical thinking and assist you in connecting theory to real-world practise.

Humanity has suffered much as a result of inequality. Regardless of our reluctance to acknowledge it, it is a reality that surrounds us. Although many people consider it to be a small problem, its impacts on the entire world show otherwise. This initiative is ideal for everyone who wishes to comprehend and overcome this terrible vice for the sake of our planet. It provides a comprehensive explanation of the topic.

Because we now live in a more developed and worldwide society where there is various thinking, tactics, and creativity that come from people in different areas of the world, the effects of intrinsic biases in us touch each and every one of us. Only our unconscious prejudices prevent us from maximising people's potential. You will learn tips on how to become self-aware of your ingrained prejudices and how to combat them in this book. This will enable you to make better decisions and open up many options.

In all facets of life, including our place of employment, it is crucial to feel appreciated as people and recognised for our accomplishments. The need to fit in is more intense in this situation. Based on how our coworkers and employer view us, we assess our value in relation to others and ourselves.

"Employees who have a strong feeling of connection to the organisation are more likely to perform well in their positions. It is one of the main forces for increased employee's belongings."

This book will also assist you in recognising the natural prejudices displayed by those with an open mind; understanding the manifestation of natural biases in the workplace and its effects; discovering how to completely overcome your unconscious prejudices. Although everyone should read this book, organisational leaders and business managers are especially encouraged to do so because these are the fields in which implicit and explicit biases are most frequently seen. The indispensable yet understandable guide for all human resource managers. This book would teach HR executives how to create a DIBs strategy that creates diverse, welcoming workplaces where everyone feels included.

"Better organisational results from creating and keeping a diverse workforce, including improved cash flow, creativity, change-readiness, and more. Even with the strongest diversity and inclusion policies and mechanisms in place, a negative encounter between one employee and another will still do damage. The goal of building an inclusive workplace is to create a setting where everyone feels comfortable speaking out, exchanging ideas, and contributing more to the team."

-Dr. Amit Das

Acknowledgements

At the outset, I will thank my family for supporting me throughout the journey of writing my book and encouraging me to live my dreams; my son has always been instrumental in giving his inspiration to complete the writing of this book. Despite the fact that I am listed as the author of this book, **"Redefining Corporate Spectrum,"** would not have been published if I had depended entirely on my own talents. Creating this book required more than anything—it took a family of dedicated and caring people who were always prepared to lend a hand.

Writing a book while working full-time is no simple task, so I'd want to express my gratitude to my amazing coworkers who act as cheerleaders in equal measure. Thank you, too, to my students and clients for your patience and unflinching support while I worked on this book!

Thank you to everyone who has listened to me argue for doing everything you can to make your life, including your work life, more progressive. I appreciate everyone's assistance throughout the process. This book would not have been possible without each of you having had an impact on my life in some manner.

Lastly, I would like to thank all the people with whom I have been associated. You gave me power. I would like to thank Notion Press for publishing my book. Finally, thank you all for gifting your time to read this book.

I'd want to convey my heartfelt appreciation to the almighty God for bestowing his blessings and being so gracious.

Creating A Positive Work Environment Through Diversity Management

"A diverse mix of voices leads to better discussions, decisions, and outcomes for everyone." — Sundar Pichai

There is much more to fostering a diverse and inclusive workplace culture than simply implementing regulations and initiatives. Understanding, respecting, and valuing differences among individuals is diversity; on the other hand, enabling equitable involvement of all workers and making them feel appreciated is inclusion. Both of these concepts must be understood by each employee and must be reflected in the organisation's activities. Given how frequently the phrase "DIBE" is used, it might be simple to overlook the many connotations of each word.

"Harnessing the power of diversity and inclusion is crucial for any organisation's viability and sustainability in the rapidly evolving business world."

A successful business is built on the pillars of (DIBE) diversity, inclusion, belonging, and equality. People who are developing company plans and goals nowadays must also be able to connect with the audience since it is so important to understand the psychology of the client. DIBE makes it feasible to do that. The previous ten years have seen a significant increase in the participation of a gender-diverse and culturally-diverse workforce, notwithstanding earlier modest progress. It began in the west as a neoteric idea and has progressively crept into workplace culture throughout the world. In today's forward-thinking business environment, practically all organisations are actively working to make diversity, inclusion, belonging, and equality (DIBE) a core component of their corporate culture. Additionally, organisations that promote an inclusive environment have seen improvements in overall performance.

Movements for inclusion and diversity in the workplace have grown over the past 20 years. This is mostly caused by the distinctions in human classification that still persist, particularly in the United States. It is clear that the trend for inclusion and diversity, particularly for people of colour, has slowed down over time. Important legislation and civil rights initiatives have, nevertheless, been put into effect.

The majority of businesses have made a significant investment in diversity because they think it will benefit their organisation and enhance their brand image. But judging whether a work environment is diverse or not involves a number of factors, both apparent and unseen. An organisation must employ a team of individuals who represent the community in which it operates in order to claim to be diverse.

"Diversity, inclusion, belonging, and equality" have become a major emphasis for corporations over the past few years (DIBE). In fact, it wouldn't be inaccurate to state that diversity, inclusion, belonging and equality have gained prominence in the workplace today. But what brought it to public attention in the first place? It's because businesses are becoming more aware of the advantages of DIBE for their operations; diversity, inclusion, belonging and equality have been linked in several studies to improved organisation success. In high-diversity contexts, inclusive teams may raise team performance by up to 30%, according to a Gartner survey.

Because the phrase "diversity and inclusion" is so well-known, it's easy to forget what it really means. Compared to their more homogenous rivals, workplaces that reflect a diverse spectrum of human experience—across gender, culture, age, sexual orientation, and other differences—are more flexible and inventive. It comes as no surprise that they perform better on measures of success, including productivity, retention, and recruiting.

Diversity in the workplace is essential for an organisation to succeed. For instance, the talent team may hire anyone with strong skills in the IT field, where working from home is typical owing to the nature of the position, whether they are a female employee looking to return to work after maternity leave, a person with a handicap, or even someone from another state. Or, to put it another way, we seek out local cuisine when we visit a new place that is not our home state in order to get a feel for the local way of life. Similarly, when people of diverse genders, races, sexual orientations, ethnicities, religions, faiths, and economic backgrounds join our organisation, it is our primary duty as an organisation to create a workplace culture that fosters a sense of belonging for everyone. For instance, if the Ganesh Chaturthi event is listed as a holiday, a team member from Maharashtra who works for a organisation in the north will feel included.

According to Indeed's most recent survey, 57% of employers are still having trouble coming up with and putting into practise the best plan. The analysis highlights an apparent disconnect between employees and their employers over how they felt about the DIBE rules in practise, suggesting that those who did support the cause may not have always been effective in achieving employee expectations. When pressed for information, none was provided. The leadership team frequently discussed the same issue. An assessment of the business's diversity and inclusion programme was spurred by this, and it revealed some improvements in the workforce's diversity but lacked a precise mechanism to gauge inclusion improvement.

Your dedication to diversity, inclusion, belonging, and equality forms the cornerstone of your culture and extends to every part of your business. You blend your unique perspectives to produce better outcomes. My clients frequently inform me that they are developing a business case for investing in DIBEs. If you don't think it's vital, I frequently question what business case will be convincing enough to explain why it's the appropriate thing to do.

Why diversity matters the most?

Businesses that welcome a variety of perspectives, skills, knowledge, and expertise into their offices frequently find that doing so helps them reduce risk, boost productivity, disrupt their industry, and spur innovation. As a result, they get a bigger piece of the future.

There are several shining instances of countries that have

valued variety and have greatly profited from creating an inclusive environment in a world where disputes over issues of race, ethnicity, and religion are frequently seen. Singapore is a prime example that springs to mind. It is a multi-ethnic society, with 76% of its citizens being Chinese, 15% being Malay, and 8% being Indian. Foreign workers make up about one-third of the whole workforce.

Foreign workers make up about one-third of the whole workforce. The country has four officially recognised languages: Chinese, Malay, Tamil, and English, and each of its citizens has a stake in the country's development. Singapore took first place in a KPMG analysis from July 2021 that ranked the greatest digital innovation clusters outside of Silicon Valley and San Francisco.

When all of this is considered, it is obvious that a connection exists between inclusion and diversity and improved performance, more creativity, and wiser judgments. Numerous studies conducted in the past ten years have unequivocally demonstrated the value of DIBE in the business setting. The renowned consulting organisation McKinsey & Co. has documented a link between organisation diversity and financial performance in a number of well-known papers.

According to a 2018 McKinsey analysis, in the top quartile of companies for gender diversity on executive teams, there is a 21% higher chance of superior profitability and a 27% higher chance of superior value creation. In a similar vein, businesses with executive teams that are ethnically and culturally diverse are 33% more likely to be profitable than their competitors.

However, as is sometimes the case, what appears to be the utmost clarity is really the most challenging to do. Everybody has prejudices that span from the brand of soap we buy at the grocery store to the people we choose to join our work team. It takes a lot of effort to cope with inclusion and diversity, and it may be quite comforting to remain with things and people that are "like us."

Diverse teams may produce excellent outcomes, but only if they can work together in a welcoming environment where everyone is free to express themselves. This fosters self-assurance, stimulates teamwork, raises understanding of cultural differences, and eventually results in the development of an all-around productive and healthy work environment. In fact, research demonstrates that diverse teams not only perform better overall but are also more creative and generally happier.

One study demonstrates how little businesses really benefit from the common approach of sending managers to diversity training to identify their prejudices, then enforcing hiring and promotion regulations and fines to modify their behaviour. You must concentrate on altering the organisational structures that hinder the success of women and people of colour. The study demonstrates how the top companies are setting the bar for new approaches to hiring, mentorship, and skill development, as well as how they are putting segregated work groups together to improve diversity. The study describes the impact of ambitious work-life initiatives.

Being an HR leader may be challenging, especially when you have to teach your employees about topics that can make some of them uneasy. Even the acronym DIBE is confusing to many people, and just because you work in HR doesn't guarantee you know what it stands for. I simply want to make sure you understand what I mean by diversity, inclusion, belonging, and equality before I get started. I would like to emphasise that inclusion is a practise and diversity is a fact.

Meanwhile, a BCG study found that businesses with diverse management teams saw a 19% gain in revenue over those with less varied teams. Therefore, if a business wants to continue to be successful over the long term, diversity and inclusion should be non-negotiable.

What DIBEs is not is a programme; it is about bringing mankind into this inner dialogue. It's not a policy, though. It's not a goal, though. Therefore, whether you're a manager or a leader, consider your team, your skills, and how transferable that talent is. A workforce that is disengaged can become involved if you consider the power of varied inclusion, belonging and, more crucially, the belonging element of culture. It would be foolish for a leader to ignore this. Therefore, getting this is essential for business success since doing so will enable you to realise both your personal and your company's full potential.

You may construct an unending list of things you wish to accomplish or avoid doing, but without a simple system for organising them, it can be quite challenging to make sense of that information. With your DIBEs programme, the same is true. You have so many options that you're not sure where to begin. First, there are things you should avoid and things you should encourage. Second, there are structural problems, such as HR procedures, and cultural problems, such as how individuals are handled.

The gender percentage gets more diversified when gender equality is prioritised while hiring teams. More diversity leads to more diversification, increased engagement, good reverberations throughout the organisation, greater satisfaction, and more.

We also know that millennials are searching for employment, a sense of purpose, and diversity. That is true.

They like to travel, have attended college, and have travelled in general. They seek out other viewpoints and experiences since they believe them to be rich. We must therefore represent what the people require. Since just 3.2% of the Fortune 500 even publish diversity statistics, how can talent now and in the future learn about who we are as a diverse society?

Additional difficulties of a political or sociological character are emerging on top of the global social trends, which, by the way, vary everywhere. As a result, the workplace can no longer tell people to leave their concerns at the door. Now it's occurring. We need to start talking right away. Our managers need to be trained on how and when to conduct this dialogue in a professional manner, but the time to do so is now.

Technological developments and the millennial attitude will have an impact on the future of diversity in the workplace. In the future, every organisation will need to have a workforce that is diverse in terms of gender, but it will also be crucial to have diversity in terms of talents, colour, culture, religion, customs, etc. Quality above quantity is the new standard. They will be able to stay connected, collaborate, and participate in the tech-driven future even when working from a distance.

In the beginning, Wipro led with gender-focused DIBE programmes to advance with their "Begin Again" for women on a career break initiative, which is one of the most brilliant programmes. They intended to accomplish good outcomes in this area and to grow and progressively improve themselves before they addressed the concerns of other disadvantaged identities. Such a well-thought-out, predetermined approach aids leaders in both identifying gaps and innovating to have a bigger effect. Most significantly, it also encourages support from the leadership.

"Honor each other's differences. Quality above quantity is the new standard."

The opportunity to express your true self at work is one of the things that a homogeneous corporate culture has mostly eliminated over time. And by fostering opportunities for self-expression, I think design may help people rediscover their connection to the workplaces they use. Self-curated team totems, for instance, might provide teams the chance to develop their connection, creativity, and authenticity while promoting awareness and diversity in the setting where they can share their strengths as a team and an individual with the rest of the workforce.

Through these, there is a chance to also increase the "office noticeboard" and, in a hybrid future, connect dispersed teams as they alternate between the office and WFH throughout the work week, providing a personal connection to teams and individuals who will return to the office after their scheduled WFH period.

Gender equality and the views of Generation Y and Z younger generations are more likely to be media and digitally aware as well as receptive to diversity and inclusion. Such characteristics will support organisations that prioritise equality, have lower structures, less bureaucracy, and greater cross-level collaboration. To increase diversity in the workplace, you can implement the following tactics:

- Establish an open, inclusive culture inside the organisation.
- Leaders to be advocates of diversity and lead the effort.

- Eliminate gender prejudice in the workplace through workshops.
- Using interventions and training, eliminate gender bias within the organisation.
- Establish women's leadership initiatives.
- Increase workplace flexibility.

It goes without saying that top management support is necessary to ignite real transformation. It is important to have the backing of the whole workplace, though. This entails having coworkers who are enthusiastic about adopting inclusive hiring practises and who are prepared to do so in their departments.

Nevertheless, real execution is harder to do in practise than in theory; here is where outside advice and assistance come in. I deliberately sought out like-minded people who are also looking at how to include DIBE (Diversity, Inclusion, Belonging, and Equality) into their organisation model for conversation. HR professionals have many possibilities to improve their plans and make sure that the execution is strategically sound since they have access to this network of advice and assistance.

People managers that embrace diversity seek out many viewpoints, pay attention to them, and treat them all equally. They also go a step further and discover hidden hurdles that others might not be aware of by questioning why specific viewpoints aren't represented. Opportunities like this promote inclusivity and result in higher-quality solutions. It is clear that an inclusive team culture and inclusive management go hand in hand.

How do we ensure that diversity is welcoming to all?

The most crucial step is to define each team member's position and responsibilities and to set clear expectations.

promoting shared understanding of roles and responsibilities. Employees who lack clarity about their tasks and get inadequate guidance may feel overburdened, bewildered, and even anxious.

In fact, a lack of knowledge might make the office a breeding ground for unhappiness. Organisations may ensure that they develop mutual understanding where members acknowledge each other's responsibilities and work in tandem with each other with respect and trust toward a similar objective by clearly planning and communicating with each team member.

It is crucial that each team member feels valued and unrebuked for their contributions. It follows that team leaders must be prepared to set up a setting where everyone is encouraged to contribute ideas, ask questions, express concerns, and make errors without fear of punishment.

"Employees won't be able to accomplish this unless they feel free to be completely themselves at work, free from any bias."

The proper training and tools are essential for teams to function well and interact, and this is especially important in the "work from home". Tools and training that are required are also essential for employees development. And by ensuring that workers are ready for any disruptions or uncertainties relating to the workplace, a culture that supports learning and growth makes a big contribution to an atmosphere that is generally healthy.

Cognitive views, education, professional experiences, life experiences, race, gender, ethnicity, sexual orientation, and many other factors are all included in the concept of diversity. Additionally, it fosters greater employee engagement and trust while expanding the talent pool. Employees develop a sense of belonging in a varied and accepting atmosphere. Employees tend to work harder and smarter, providing higher-quality work and positively affecting business returns when they feel more engaged at work.

How to Change corporate policies to promote diversity at work?

At the organisational level, there are businesses today that support diversity, but they don't foster inclusivity. Despite hiring workers from a variety of backgrounds, the organisational structure prevents the employees from expressing their actual selves, which deters individuals from wanting to work for the organisations longer. Researchers and thought leaders are, nevertheless, steadily bringing about change in this area. In most organisations, it is still in its infancy, but it will soon be in charge of work culture.

What can be done now to keep workers from varied backgrounds on board? The first step in fostering gender and cultural diversity is implementing an equal employment opportunity policy. Another important factor is a set of policies for improving the gender split. There have also been several discussions on gender wage discrepancies. To guarantee talent retention, reasonable remuneration, prizes, promotions, rewards, insurance coverage, etc. are helpful.

According to statistics, 30% of the population of the United States is currently foreign-born or has immigrant ancestry.

We must accept variety and use methods to harness our differences for beneficial outcomes if we are to have a functioning society, a productive workplace, and a productive society. Because we now live in a more developed and worldwide society where unique thinking, ideas, and creativity emerge from people in different areas of the world, the inherent biases in each of us affect each and every one of us. Only our unconscious prejudices prevent us from maximising people's potential.

We also require inclusive leadership in our communities and organisations because it is the most significant aspect of our lives. Just as the brain in the head serves as the primary organ for the control and regulation of bodily functions in other parts of the body, leaders play a crucial role in all aspects of human existence. Failures in leadership are unquestionably to blame for the failures and deterioration in our society.

The business climate in India has seen a reformist change over time. More businesses setting up shop in the country's outlying regions has given competent people living in Tier-3, Tier-4, and even underdeveloped regions new career opportunities. Additionally, it has permitted local hiring drives where businesses have hired people from various societal segments.

Contrary to the decades-old strict workplace culture, more organisations are moving toward creating an inclusive workplace where people of all origins, creeds, faiths, and cultures may work together. A McKinsey study found that organisations that prioritise gender, cultural, and ethnic diversity at work outperform their rivals in terms of profitability.

According to the data, there is a statistically significant link between improved financial performance and a more diversified leadership team. Companies with higher gender diversity had a 15% higher likelihood of posting financial returns above the national sector median. Financial returns above the national sector median were 35% more probable for businesses in the top quartile of racial/ethnic diversity.

Companies were statistically less likely to generate above-average financial returns when they were in the bottom quartile for both gender and ethnicity/race than the dataset's average organisation (that is, they were not just not leading, they were lagging). The outcomes vary by nation and sector. In the US, for example, businesses with management teams and boards that were 10% more diverse in terms of gender and ethnicity had EBIT that was 1.1 percent higher; in the UK, businesses with the same level of diversity had EBIT that was 5.8 percent higher.

Furthermore, the inconsistent performance of businesses operating in the same sector and nation suggests that diversity functions as a competitive differentiator, shifting market share in favour of businesses with greater diversity.

Variations by nation demonstrate that the threshold for competitive differentiation keeps going up. For instance, in the US, the association between ethnic/racial diversity and superior financial success is still linear. In fact, ethnic/racial diversity in the US has a greater influence on financial success than gender diversity, notwithstanding prior efforts to boost the participation of women in the upper echelons of business, which have already produced fruitful outcomes. Contrarily, in the UK, the biggest performance improvement in the global dataset was correlated with more gender diversity on the executive team. From the standpoint of an industry, some perform better than others in terms of ethnic/racial diversity and gender diversity. A organisation or industry did not rank in the top quartile for either metric.

The study's highlighted correlation—not a causal link—between diversity and performance is a correlation only. Despite this critical distinction, the findings allow for plausible theories about what motivates businesses with diverse executive teams and boards to perform better. It makes sense—and has been proven in previous research, as we've mentioned—that more diverse businesses are better equipped to attract top personnel, as well as to enhance their focus on customers, employee happiness, and decision-making, which creates a positive feedback loop that boosts profits. That in turn implies that diversity outside of gender, ethnicity, race, and sexual orientation, as well as diversity of experience, such as a global mindset and cultural fluency, is also likely to bring some level of competitive advantage for organisations that are able to attract and retain such diverse talent.

Because of how linked and globalised our society has grown, diversity is important. It shouldn't be surprising that organisations and businesses with greater diversity are performing better. Most organisations, including McKinsey, have work to do in order to fully capitalise on the opportunity that a more diverse leadership team represents. In particular, there is more work to be done on the talent pipeline: luring in, nurturing, mentoring, sponsoring, and retaining the upcoming generations of global leaders at all levels of the organisation. Given the predicted rising returns that diversity will provide, it is preferable to invest now rather than later since winners will continue to move ahead and laggards will continue to fall behind.

There are several ways for businesses to step up their diversity and inclusion initiatives. Several businesses provide mentorship and coaching programmes to help ensure that women and minorities have an equal chance at success. For instance, the German corporation Siemens, which manufactures industrial equipment, has a programme called "Women and their Path within the Company". It employs coaching, mentoring, and training to assist women in achieving leadership positions. Such initiatives can improve the retention of bright women. In one of my own studies, I discovered that placing women in high-potential pools also reduced turnover—but only if they had other women in positions of authority above them, such as a female manager.

The research strongly suggests that having some women in high leadership positions inside a company is crucial for sending a message to other female employees that there are opportunities for progression. Another method to enhance inclusion is by eliminating a significant institutional prejudice that makes it harder for women to compete in the workforce. Someone's family. Companies like Colgate Palmolive include work-life initiatives into their talent strategy, such as flexible work schedules or condensed workweeks. To encourage work-life balance, they provide emergency in-home childcare for dependents and financial aid for tuition. Thanks to all of these initiatives, women may now bring their whole selves to work.

However, they're also helpful for drawing in and keeping millennials, who frequently desire more work freedom. Employer resource groups, or ERGs, are another feature common to most businesses. referred to as affinity groups. Diversity councils have replaced ERGs at other businesses, including Deloitte. All of these organisations exist to provide social assistance by facilitating connections between people who have common interests.

However, they frequently provide some kind of instrumental assistance as well. They might provide access to specialised mentorship or training programmes, a channel for the ERG to reach high leadership, or even a mechanism to have one's opinion heard. Using a varied, multidisciplinary, or cross-functional task force to address an organisational problem is one concept I particularly enjoy. Even while diversity isn't the main goal, these do really bring different individuals together and improve inclusion. Medtronic is one of my favourite brands. One of the biggest medical equipment firms in the world is this one. The programme is known as "culture circles". Teams strive to resolve a problem within the organisation, and then they assemble for a large competition to determine the best solutions. These cultural circles are really engaging, as I can attest from my attendance. The cultural challenge for the most recent year was to boost productivity.

"Strength lies in differences, not in similarities." –
Stephen Covey

Employers must also be ready to empower everyone to have open discussions and to provide them with the information and tools necessary to create the psychological safety for such discussions. Companies are promoting diversity and inclusion in a variety of ways. Others place a stronger emphasis on inclusion, enabling people to bring their entire selves to work, while others place an emphasis on diversity, expanding the number of underrepresented groups. Let's discuss initiatives to promote diversity.

Increasing the depth of recruitment efforts to obtain a more diversified talent pool is the simplest sell for a business. There is no indication that anyone is gaining an undue advantage from this. However, if you examine your application statistics and discover that your candidate pool is not diverse, you may be able to make a difference by simply expanding your recruitment efforts.

Consider this: how do you often learn about new
positions?

If the majority of your company's employees are white men, then so will be the majority of their networks. In actuality, our networks resemble ourselves quite a bit. Therefore, we need to figure out how to connect with those who aren't generally part of our network. This can entail hiring from historically black universities or more diversely represented businesses. Not only would this boost diversity, but it would also raise the calibre of your candidate pool. If you just hire white guys from the 31% of the population in the US, for instance, you won't be getting the greatest talent available.

In fact, you're getting the top talent by enlarging your talent pool. You're making art. From the whole population, you are selecting the greatest individuals. Surprisingly, however, just 10% of international businesses claim to be making such an effort to increase their talent pool. Therefore, this could be an excellent solution for your business. The second thing that businesses frequently do is search for strategies to lessen prejudice throughout the hiring process.

I'll give you an illustration of bias: Numerous studies have been carried out by experts in the US and Canada using real resumes submitted for real jobs. They are false resumes, and the applicant's sex or race is the only difference. They discover that a CV that is exactly the same except for the name to be that of a white male increases the likelihood of receiving a callback and increases the beginning wage.

Our prejudices are powerful, and it may be quite challenging to get past them. Therefore, removing all identifying information from resumes is one technique to eliminate the possibility of prejudice. Blinding the selecting process is what this is. According to research by the consulting firm Gap Jumpers, when standard resume screening is used, 80% of candidates who advance to the first round of interviews are white, male, and physically fit individuals from prestigious colleges. Blind selection yielded a result of 40%. By establishing clear criteria before you analyse candidate applications or conduct interviews, you may also lessen prejudice. Google, which was renowned for its eccentric interview questions, has actually abandoned them in favour of more formal tests with clearly stated success criteria. Additionally, organisations like PWC, Facebook, Coca-Cola, and Lockheed-Martin provide training on unconscious bias to help individuals become aware of their prejudices.

"There are several approaches to boosting diversity. These are but a few of the ones that businesses utilise the most. increasing talent pool diversity and subsequently reducing prejudice in the hiring process."

Human resource professionals, managers, and team leaders must learn how to have thoughtful discussions about potentially divisive subjects, including race, religion, and gender. Many businesses encourage employees members to bring their whole selves to work. since they are aware of their increased engagement, productivity, and innovation. Employees are welcome to bring difficulties and worries pertaining to significant facets of their identity with them when they accept this offer.

Why and how to hire broadly finding qualified, competent applicants is a standard human resources task that frequently takes place?

Building a culture of responsibility throughout the organisation—and not just among HR managers—should be a goal for organisations. All organisational levels should take ownership of and play a key role in fostering an inclusive culture. Since each component of the workplace ecosystem has a specific function to perform, it is obvious that everyone is accountable for inclusion. HR managers, however, are a theme that runs through the entire organisation and has a significant impact.

One method that executives and HR specialists may use to start a transformation in the organisation is through inclusive recruiting. It goes beyond simply hiring individuals from underrepresented backgrounds to simply checking a box. It is a procedure that actively values diversity and welcomes a variety of traits and viewpoints that applicants might offer the organisation.

More significantly, it enables organisations to access an untapped pool of skilled people and translates to doing good over the long run. These include elderly people, ex-offenders, disabled people, and single moms who are returning to work. People with disabilities might perform tasks that were unaffected by their impairments. We had a deaf-mute employee who cleaned glasses, for instance, and a wheelchair-bound employee who operated the phone with one arm. Furthermore, this is only the tip of the iceberg. An attitude change is needed for inclusive hiring.

The traditional role of human resources frequently entails identifying the most qualified individuals who are both successful and efficient. Today, though, that has expanded to include the strategic implementation of diversity, equity, and inclusion in the workplace. This is because it is understood that these efforts will not only have a positive, long-term impact on the organisation and its bottom line but will also be a crucial component of its ongoing efforts to do good.

Seniors are very good at mentoring younger employees, especially if they have held the position for a long time.

These duties include those related to providing customer service in areas like in-room dining, serving as lobby ambassadors, and cleaning common spaces.

One of the greatest bets for any HR strategy is to make it a business necessity by highlighting not just the advantages it offers to its workers but also the organisation over the long run. But not all businessmen share this opinion.

While the indirect connection between DIBE and good commercial outcomes cannot be disputed, organisations must prioritise "doing the right thing." There are many different ways that individuals debate, plan, and work together, but regardless of the statistics on workplace diversity, inclusiveness, and equality are those values that must be respected. And this is true, particularly in the employment sector, where employment opportunities are equally available to members of all communities. However, what organisations do following the diversity-driven hiring process is crucial.

While the C-suite establishes DIBE as a business priority and allots resources and financing, HR is in charge of putting policies and procedures into place, and workers are in charge of being open-minded to different points of view and building an inclusive culture. While all three of these parties are significant players, leaders at all levels are crucial for developing an inclusive workplace because they frequently make choices on recruiting, growth, progress, and engagement.

Managers implement this on the ground while leadership sets the tone at the top. Goals for diversity, equity, and inclusion are incorporated into managers' yearly performance targets to help them be held accountable and to motivate them to establish inclusive teams. Diverse representation is necessary but not sufficient.

Our managers play a crucial part in establishing the ideal workplace by promoting equity rather than merely equality. The organisation supports its managers with regular training and coaching sessions on unconscious bias; recognising, understanding, and appreciating differences; and leading inclusively, stressing that managers are also responsible for fostering a sense of belonging within teams, so people feel included and their talents and experiences are valued while differences are celebrated.

A secure environment for the community's members may be created with the aid of people managers. There is no denying that DIBE is a process and not an instant transformation. The journey also offers a unique set of lessons because not everyone is familiar with the nuances of the several distinct segments that modern businesses serve. Collaborative inclusion is made possible through encouraging inclusive behaviour.

While it is true that everyone has a responsibility to promote inclusiveness, people managers are crucial in spreading this message throughout the different organisational levels, departments, and individuals. I believe that everyone at work has a duty to foster a secure and welcoming workplace, not just HR managers. Managers of people should set an example, nevertheless. Every person in the organisation has a responsibility to "walk the talk" in order to serve as coaches or mentors. Up to 87% of the time, inclusive teams choose superior business strategies. And judgments taken and carried out by diverse teams produced results that were 60% better.

Given these facts, it is clear why there is still so much space for improvement. Here are three crucial areas of action that can assist organisations accomplish what we refer to as a DIBE transformation in the workplace if they are having trouble deciding how to move forward.

Start by getting the right people on the bus, the wrong people off the bus, and the right people seated, as Jim Collins advised in his book "Good to Great." The other factors really don't matter if you don't have a solid talent base—and to me, that implies a diversified one. For example, if you don't have any diversity to begin with, you can't promote inclusion or decrease turnover among your varied talent. Here are a few suggestions to enhance recruiting and selection so you can hire a team that is more diverse.

First, in your employment materials, stress the importance of diversity. Make sure the language you use in your job materials doesn't deter particular groups from applying and that it reflects the kind of organisation you want to be. Next, consider the younger generations. Young women are more likely to have graduated from college than they were in the past, and young people throughout the world are generally growing more varied, both racially and culturally. By developing internships that prioritise hiring students from varied backgrounds or hiring entry-level employees from more diverse schools, you may take advantage of this rise in diversity. Third, hire people outside of your current networks.

We are aware that our networks resemble ourselves when it comes to hiring non-entry level workers, so you must develop strategies to attract talent that doesn't resemble us. Expand your perspective on the sources of potential hires. You can look at sectors that are more diversified than your own but yet need the same set of skills. This reasoning continues up to the board level. Take these measures into account throughout the screening process if you can attract a more varied candidate pool. Make sure your selection tools are impartial to begin with. The simplest approach to doing this is to blind applications, which involves erasing applicants' names.

To ensure that your standards don't alter based on who you're interviewing, you can also be certain that you specify your recruiting criteria in advance and then evaluate candidates using those criteria. Second, make sure your short list of candidates includes at least two women or people of colour. In such a case, return to recruitment. Third, make sure the people you interview are varied as well. Fourth, after you have a list of suitable applicants based on your interviews, I advise selecting the candidate that not only provides a fresh viewpoint but is also obviously fully qualified given that they made it this far in the selection process.

Instead of only choosing the individual with the highest score, you may choose people who fit your needs. So, you'll evaluate your previous job listings as your initial step. Are there any ways you might make those better to draw in a more varied candidate pool? After that, be sure to include those modifications in your subsequent posting. You are already implementing your DIBEs programme by doing this.

I believe that culture is the key to properly onboarding and managing millennials. Therefore, I appreciate that it is finally getting the attention it deserves. It's difficult to conceive why someone would agree to work a job for 40, 50, or more hours a week if they aren't obtaining something essential from their surroundings.

The ideals of a workplace, behavioural standards, beliefs, actions, and words all contribute to the culture of a organisation, which is what I mean when I say what it's like to work there. And I believe that a organisation's ability to define its culture and communicate it well is quite strong. Many people begin by speaking with their employees. What are their reasons for choosing you, staying with you, and recommending your business to their friends and contacts? And as time passes, you may begin to see certain trends. The culture is made up of these. They frequently contribute to the so-called employee value proposition, which explains why a certain employee would choose to work for your business. And I believe that it may be a fantastic opportunity for management, on the one hand. It's a great recruitment strategy to create a culture that genuinely motivates individuals.

On the other hand, many managers discover that they don't really like the culture they've established. People frequently believe that culture simply kind of occurs, but in my opinion, genuinely great organisations are formed with purpose. As a result, I believe that managers who are perhaps engaging in a culture exercise and realising that they may not be fostering the kind of work environment they'd like have a chance to really listen to the feedback they're receiving from their teams and employees and reflect on how they can change things and what kind of organisation they want to create.

Because, in the end, highly competent individuals are searching for opportunities and aren't only comparing organisations based on pay and benefits. They are weighing them based on the culture and the working environment. The ways in which people and businesses interact with one another have undoubtedly changed significantly, and for every business with a more conventional procedure, there have been some quite intriguing exceptions.

I've observed businesses inviting candidates into problem-solving sessions rather than conducting traditional interviews, which may occasionally feel a touch monotonous. I believe it would be extremely nice if businesses paid employees when it was possible. Therefore, they will say, "We want you to come in; we'll pay you for an hour, and we'll really have you problem-solve with a handful of team members." Once more, I believe that many businesses are afraid to stray from the norm, but those that do frequently discover that doing so results in their hiring individuals who are really innovative.

If you could explain to millennials at onboarding how what they're going to do ties in with the organisation's bigger picture, I believe that because millennials in general are exposed to a wide range of options, they are particularly looking for businesses that will support their development and offer them opportunities for professional progress. You can really lay out what you're going to learn and what you're going to get out of this position during onboarding, and managing millennials is all about providing them with criticism while also listening to it, because I believe many people nowadays expect to have a role in the decision-making process.

There are several reasons why diversity in the workplace is becoming increasingly essential. In the 20th century, having similar views was advantageous. It now represents a risk in the twenty-first century. One type of intellect cannot solve all of society's problems. It can't rely just on one viewpoint. There is no longer the notion that particular individuals in specific regions of the world have exclusive knowledge of the answers needed to address global concerns.

Therefore, if nations, businesses, or individuals wish to develop, they must assess their capacity to withstand change. Because if we can't open ourselves up to new ideas, if we can't let others challenge our worldviews, if we can't allow our minds to grow, then we're a dying breed. Therefore, we need to think about diversity in terms that are much, much larger than we have traditionally thought of it, not just in terms of gender but also in terms of how we approach and view situations.

How diversity is closely correlated with business growth?

Nearly all organisational jobs, from leaders and innovators to organisation executives, require merit, which is paving the way for an inclusive culture. The majority of businesses with target markets in the rural sector have profited in recent years from a diversified employees.

Take the banking sector's Business Correspondent division, for instance. Recruiting workers from the neighbourhood is a terrific way to build a varied and inclusive clientele. There is more possibility for relatability when there is a sizable workforce from the same neighbourhood. As a result, customers develop trust and loyalty towards the brand as a result of this.

Furthermore, it seems to make sense that businesses that prioritise customer service would have a varied clientele. This is especially true in India, where a diverse range of cultures, socioeconomic classes, faiths, genders, ethnicities, and even races coexist. In light of this, an inclusive team of representatives in a organisation is better able to comprehend, clarify, and establish a solid rapport between a brand and its clients.

People who are developing organisation plans and goals nowadays must also be able to connect with the audience since it is so important to understand the psychology of the client. An amalgamation of workers with various backgrounds is practical in this situation. A workforce that is diverse has its own unique set of experiences, viewpoints, and ideas.

ITC's key values of Trusteeship, Customer Focus, Respect for People, Excellence, Innovation, and Nation Orientation include the principles of inclusion and diversity, making them a way of life for us. Talking about DIBEs across nations with varied political, social, and cultural subtleties is not always simple. We have made diversity and inclusion one of our key organisational priorities. Even though we are spread out throughout the globe, we get together as a team to celebrate our interconnectedness and cultural variety. Our worldwide plans generally respond to local needs. In both business and geographic leadership positions, women are a major factor. DIBE transcends issues of gender, race, and ethnicity. However, studies have revealed that just one in three workers believe senior executives actively promote workplace inclusiveness and open dialogue on diversity.

Large data-set studies have an apparent drawback, they can only demonstrate a correlation between diversity and improved performance, not an actual causation. Consider another often referenced study between 1985 and 2008, 1,500 research and scientific publications were published by the US National Bureau of Economic Research. People who dislike stepping outside of their comfort zones on DIBE issues frequently point out that studies like the one from McKinsey above only show a correlation, not a cause-and-effect relationship. A little thinking exercise should be sufficient to explain why such a link might exist. After all, a organisation would do well to have teams with a range of skills, expertise, information, and viewpoints if it plans to create and sell products or services globally.

The study discovered that scholars' contributions to science were less the more homogeneous their origins were. Papers with stronger homophily typically appear in journals with lower impact factors and get fewer citations than other papers. Even though they discovered that inclusive decision-making produces better results, the white paper concluded that diverse teams were "more likely to experience operational friction while implementing them." But the rewards might be significant for businesses that can get beyond this obstacle. Very diverse teams were twice as likely to both make better decisions and also provide results that met or surpassed expectations. When such individuals dispute with one another, it forces everyone to work and think more diligently. In contrast to uniformity, diversity stimulates us to behave cognitively. In a variety of settings, people do better socially and cognitively.

As a result, companies are strengthened locally, and more customer-focused goods and services are created. According to research, diverse and inclusive teams make better judgments than non-diverse teams and decision-makers acting alone.

DIBEs (Diversity, Inclusion, Belonging and Equality) are more than simply trendy terms. The productivity and wellbeing of employees can be significantly impacted by DIBE initiatives. Consider the finest group you have ever been a member of. In that group, you likely felt that everyone respected and cared for you. That is the environment that encourages collaboration, creativity, and development. Therefore, the answer is yes, irrespective of your industry, sector, or nation. Your organisation may benefit from diversity, inclusion, and belonging, which can enhance how you work, invent, and flourish. The same issue is being posed by IT businesses, colleges, local governments, national parks, and presumably mountain research stations as they all rise to the occasion.

How do you begin if you want to do something different, if you want to alter things in a way that welcomes new individuals, new concepts, and new cultural values?

You can start a movement regardless of your position—whether you're the CEO of a corporation, a college intern, or anything in between. But regardless of your position, one of the most beneficial things you can do is clearly define the business case for diversity, inclusion, and belonging in your organisation before you start developing a DIBEs programme. You might not have access to all the information about your own organisation, but you can look up some information online about the value of belonging, inclusion, and diversity in organisations like yours. Consider what would be important to the CEO or president of your organisation. reputation, revenue, and employees retention. Make a straightforward business case to investigate belonging, equality, diversity, and inclusion. Make a straightforward business case to investigate belonging, diversity, equality, and inclusion.

For instance, if there are a lot of millennials working for your organisation, you may provide data on how important diversity is to this generation. You might provide information on how diversity enables you to access a larger consumer base if you work in sales. Decide the business need for diversity, inclusiveness, and belonging in your particular organisation today, even if you're the lone wolf just starting out on this route, to improve diversity, inclusion, belonging, and equality. Your first step in determining what you require in order to experience the advantages you desire will be to take this action.

In a organisation with a varied culture, emotional intelligence (EQ) is essential. Due to their empathy for their subordinates, those with higher EQ tend to be better leaders. Their team is motivated by their self-awareness, outstanding communication skills, empathy, and ability to control emotions. As stated in Deloitte Insights, "According to our model, engagement spans five main areas: meaningful work and jobs; management practises and behaviours; the work environment; chances for development and progress; and confidence in leadership." Continuous feedback, team-building exercises, employee surveys, and methods to make meetings fun for everyone are a few ways that EQ may support diversity and inclusion. Open communication between the executives and the employees will only encourage people to express themselves freely and function as pillars for businesses with a diverse range of cultures. " This study demonstrates that both emotional intelligence and work-life balance combined promote organisational success and develop competitive advantage for organisations, "as stated plainly in A Study on Emotional Intelligence at Work."

According to research, inclusive cultures are six times more likely to foster innovation and agility, and eight times more likely to provide superior financial results. However, the strongest business argument is that individuals function at their best when they can be themselves at work and thrive, not in spite of who they are, but precisely because of who they are.

Keeping out of the dialogue or only having it if it benefits the bottom line is just not an option for today's multigenerational workforces, who expect their workplaces and executives to take the lead on inclusion. Therefore, change the dialogue from asking "What is the business case?" to asking "How can this make us a stronger organisation."

We are able to offer distinctive goods and services that are competitively superior and reach a far wider variety of clients thanks to the input of mixed communities of workers and partners in our value creation processes.

By encouraging an atmosphere of empowerment and inclusion and using our different human resources, we celebrate the individuality of each person and help them achieve holistic growth and lasting competitive advantages. The following aspirational goals have been created by us to direct our journey and show our dedication:

Create a culture that is welcoming to all workers and provides them with a fair opportunity to reach their potential. Achieve 65% female diversity, including in operational positions, and 40% at the leadership level to achieve equal gender representation across management levels.

Putting employees first Encourage deep adoption by identifying unique organisational and personnel concerns, developing an appropriate DIBE strategy, and communicating this to all levels of the organisation.e practises are used to enhance our commitment to diversity, equality, belonging, and inclusion.

Our procedures and regulations give workers fair and equitable access to all of the organisation's possibilities. In line with our dedication to merit-based hiring, we have the greatest tools and procedures to make sure we have access to the widest pool of diverse applicants. A data-focused approach Utilise data to identify particular gaps in decision-making, diversity, and employee fairness to create customised programmes for various corporate sectors. In order to understand what works at different levels of the organisation, we are monitoring various projects across various shareholders.

Integrate DIBE into current hiring and operational procedures: To integrate DIBE and build long-term value around collaboration, innovation, and growth, talent management procedures like succession planning, hiring, and performance management should be the first place to start. These processes are some of the most prone to prejudice.

But DIBE is, quite rightly, not merely about a feel-good element or a moral obligation. It should be obvious by now that it has the potential to provide organisations with a critical advantage in order to succeed and perform better in a globalised, hypercompetitive environment. It seems to make sense that the CEO drives the agenda for inclusion and diversity at the top businesses.

In addition to ethnicity, nationality, handicapping, and sexual orientation, gender is one facet of diversity. In order to address this, we have set goals to hire 1% of people with special needs, 2% of LGBTQ employees, a healthy geo-mix, and people from J&K, the Northeastern states, and economically disadvantaged backgrounds (Indian context).

"Leaders with a growth mentality will determine whether organisations develop and stay competitive, or stagnate and go extinct, with inclusive leadership being the only viable option. The competence qualities of the culture builders who will shape our world's future are discussed, along with issues of prejudice and balance."

According to the impact of diversity on groups, more diversity is linked to improved collaboration and idea generation. By having new talent and innovative ideas, it gives businesses the chance to spot the newest trends. It serves as a major motivation for employees members, lowers absenteeism, and fosters a sense of community in both real and virtual offices. Employee involvement is crucial for developing an empowering organisation culture. Employees who interact with individuals from various cultures learn about other cultures and feel appreciated. In order to advance DIBE, business conglomerates are establishing diversity councils, hosting webinars, panel discussions, learning and development (L&D) modules, seminars, catch-up sessions, and management training programmes. Looking inside, it's crucial to remember that during both pandemic waves, logistics specialists risked their lives while working against the clock to bring happiness, health, and safety to our doorstep. In such a situation, it is essential to provide employees' wellbeing and mental health with greater attention than ever before. An ideal gender balance in the workforce ensures that decision-making, innovation, creativity, and knowledge-sharing processes run smoothly inside a business. To secure their growth in the current environment, businesses must carefully reorganise their employment policies. For many years, the ratio of frontline employees has been skewed towards one gender.

You may put the culture you have worked so hard to create into action in a few different ways: sharing the decision-making process may lead to more inclusion from siloed departments, team development, and novel ideas that you would not have thought of on your own. Be adaptable. Be sympathetic and cognizant of the requirements of the employee. Being flexible doesn't require being overly forgiving, but it also doesn't require being very punitive either. For instance, a new mom could need to stay at home, or someone who might be ill might be allowed to work from home. Recognise that everyone has various expectations for their jobs based on their individual professional aspirations. You will comprehend the various aims in tandem with your communication with the team members. Make an effort to acknowledge them and assist them in accomplishing it.

A genuine mentor like that system of recognition: It has been demonstrated that systems that acknowledge and reward employees for their efforts are more productive and significantly contribute to the development of stronger teams. According to the research from the White Paper: Hacking Diversity with Inclusive Decision-Making, "Up to 87% of the time, inclusive teams make better judgments." Teams that use an inclusive method get conclusions twice as quickly and in half the sessions. Diverse teams' decisions and execution led to 60% greater results. DIBE has countless more advantages for creating a positive workplace culture in any corporation. And the results of putting these simple measures into action may significantly impact a organisation's earnings. By giving the team a place to celebrate one another and themselves and to be more inclusive of one another, DIBE helps the organisation stand out by fostering a healthy work environment.

"Diverse and inclusive businesses are seen as bringing innovation and changing the sector with strategic consequences, in addition to being a coveted trait among potential workers."

Implementing DIBE can benefit from a needs assessment of the organisation.

- What is your current workforce make-up?

- Where are you located globally?
- What products are available?
- Where are your clients located globally?
- What industry do you work in?
- What kind of employee benefits policy can you bring to the workplace in order to manage a diverse workforce, etc.?

The HR executive must have a clear vision and aim before implementing such events in a business. DIBE implementation is chosen depending on the diverse workforce. Therefore, assessing your workforce's strength is important before beginning.

If an organisation is focusing on equal women's participation, then policies and benefits specific to women should be included in the organisation. Examples include maternity leave, menstrual policy, leave, reimbursement for fertility treatment, on-site childcare, surrogacy policies, POSH committee, and transportation for late night shift or those women who work night shift, as well as restricted holidays for festivals like Karrwa Chauth.

According to a recent survey by the diversity and inclusion organisation Avtar Group, recruiting for diverse candidates in 2020 increased by 32% this year compared to 23% last year. According to the survey, the average percentage of women in the top 100 organisations increased from 33% in 2019 to 34% in 2020.

Additionally, the percentage of women on corporate boards has climbed to 27%. Women are a talent pool, but they are the group most negatively impacted by the epidemic because they must balance work and family responsibilities. Due to their social and other duties, they were unable to go to work, but the DIBE event made a significant contribution to moving women from their homes to workplaces through hybrid working arrangements or long-term work from home settings. These advantages will foster a feeling of acceptance, together with laws that support women's equality. The first step in putting a diversity plan into practise is to have a well-defined talent acquisition policy. This can help you decide what kinds of diversity factors should be taken into account when planning personnel.

However, it is reassuring to know that there are now significantly more women working in the logistics sector. In 2020 research from Gartner, women now make up 39% of full-time workers in supply chain roles, up from 35% in 2016. Companies are dedicated to altering women's futures at work over time by offering them options for upskilling and educational training. Additionally, they are assisting them in breaking the stereotype of "male-dominated" professions and preparing them for leadership roles. Additionally, in order to make sure that both existing and potential workers are aware of the racial makeup of their organisation, executives perform yearly monitoring and diversity audits.

As thought leaders in this field, it is our responsibility to develop the best methodologies to align our organisations with our DIBE objectives, ensuring that every member has the opportunity for 360-degree growth and wellbeing through equitable work distribution, ongoing communication with their employees, and collaborative opportunities.

Of course, there is a better approach, according to goal-setting philosophy. If I'm being more practical, I may aim to contact a buddy once per week or once per month. This reasoning also applies to your DIBEs programme. You must clarify your meaning, establish a target, and track your progress. Knowing that setting objectives has the biggest influence on change among all diversity initiatives is crucial. Therefore, let's first discuss how to define demographic targets before moving on to cultural goals. If you know what you need, setting demographic targets is rather simple.

For instance, you could want 15% of your new hires to be individuals with disabilities, 10% of them to be veterans, or 30% of your whole employees to be people of colour. Goals based on turnover or promotion rates are another option. If you expect 30% of your promotions to the next level to be made to women, if you have 30% of female mid-level managers, Even obtaining a spot on a list of the greatest companies to work for might be a goal. One additional thing to consider is that you don't simply need to create outcome objectives, such as "by the end of the year, 80% of our employees will be engaged," or "we'll see a 20% boost in our engagement ratings," which are the results of your efforts.

However, you might also establish participation targets, such as determining what proportion of individuals you want to enrol in a volunteer training course. Or how many women should be involved in a mentoring program? To make sure that your message is conveyed correctly, I also like to include awareness goals. In other words, are individuals even aware that a mentorship programme exists? Let's now discuss establishing cultural objectives. Culture objectives have to do with how people are made to feel by your organisation. I'll grant that it might be challenging to put a number on this, but how will you ever know whether you were successful if you can't describe your objectives? Or even how success appears? Many organisations I've dealt with use objectives that relate to where they want the organisation to go. For instance, they could want 80% of their employees to be engaged. Unless you have benchmarking data on the survey measures you use, Consider a target that you can achieve using the DIBs Program. What are your plans for the upcoming week, month, or year? Simply defining a goal for your DIBs programme increases your chances of success.

Since organisations often never assess their accomplishments, I always keep this in mind while evaluating DIBE projects. Even though they seldom ever look into which particular aspects of the programmes are succeeding as well as which individuals were If you don't design your DIBEs programme with this sort of review in mind, it can be very challenging to do. The concept is that you must first determine the program's objectives before listing them. What is the precise work that must be completed? Who is in charge of carrying it out? What time window is there for implementing it? How will you gauge your progress in light of your starting point and objectives? Your objectives can include, for instance, broadening the diversity of your application pool. The activities you've identified as necessary to achieve this goal are sending recruiters to historically black universities, updating your website, adding a diversity statement to your job postings, and placing the onus of duty on the head of recruitment. You must come up with a measurement strategy by the end of the year. Your application pool's baseline composition was 80% white and 80% male, and your target composition may be 30% people of colour and 30% women.

In terms of analysing the true efficacy of DIBEs initiatives, most businesses fall short. Don't you want to know whether it was successful after you have just put in so much effort to bring about change? After that, you might reallocate resources from the unsuccessful activities to the successful ones. Measure your progress along the way to make adjustments before it's too late and to make sure you're on track to reach your objectives. Consider doing focus groups or employee interviews as part of your assessments to get their opinions on the programme and their perceptions of the improvements that have resulted. Make sure your modifications don't alienate other team members and spark a backlash while also boosting diversity, inclusiveness, and a sense of belonging. Managers have admitted that they will consciously recruit individuals who lack the necessary skills. They will tick a box if HR asks them to, but they don't support it. That is an illustration of blowback. The crucial thing to remember is that you must constantly analyse the state of your DIBEs programme and gauge its effectiveness. Consider a few approaches to evaluate the performance of your diversity, inclusion, and belonging initiatives. And in reality, by doing this, you might be able to truly focus on what you want to achieve.

Therefore, go out on a fact-finding quest to begin your adventure. Importantly, evaluate your organisation's needs at this point. It is simple to leap to offering answers to DIBE's difficulties, but this is truly useless until you are aware of the challenges your business is dealing with. Make sure you have the information necessary to describe a need, then develop a solution to meet that need. What type of data are you looking for initially, though? Start by checking internal demographic information. Verify whether the data for your organisation is accessible via the intranet or internet.

Otherwise, HR ought to have access to all of this data as they require it for their EEO reports. However, if no one offers it to you, especially if your organisation is small, you can really obtain the data on your own. Simply count the population to determine your total. Age, handicap, ethnicity or national origin, gender and gender identity, race, religion, and veteran status are the considerations that are protected by federal law. However, you should also consider evaluating other forms of diversity, such as sexual orientation and family status.

In order to comprehend various departments, locations, and, most crucially, organisational levels, you should stratify the data as well. Is there diversity in your organisation's entry-level positions but not in the executive positions at the top? You want to know facts like this, right? Then, find out how diverse other businesses that are comparable to yours are by looking at their statistics. Then, find out how diverse other businesses that are comparable to yours are by looking at their statistics. Big businesses are becoming far more open about their demographic information. Therefore, if you visit the websites of your peer groups, you may check if they provide any information on the demographics of their organisation. You may also think about researching some statistics for your industry as a whole. The proportion of recent graduates who are women in engineering may be important information if you're trying to attract more female engineers. Your benchmarks will be set with the use of this data. Next, collect information on the organisational culture and employee satisfaction.

Many companies use surveys to get this kind of data, but you can also conduct focus groups and interviews. Look for instances when people felt excluded, there was prejudice perceived against them, or they felt truly supported. Are you attempting to determine whether or not everyone feels included and a part of the group? If other organisations are performing well in terms of diversity, investigate what they are doing to achieve that success by visiting their websites. What are some of their diversity or human resources policies that you might use? How do they find, choose, and keep talent? Does there exist a mentorship programme just for women? You may begin to identify some areas where improvement is possible after you have all the information on where your gaps are and how your business stacks up against other businesses.

To participate in board meetings and learn how they are run. How do we pose inquiries? How do we decide what to do? In order to expose the younger generation—both men and women—to what occurs, opportunities must be provided. ' Because if we have to wait till younger people are at a level where they can be invited to join boards, they will have lost out on a lot of years where they might have been developed, given the tools they needed, and prepared to be productive board members.We must understand that the people we interact with on a daily basis—both at work and in our personal lives—are a constant source of learning opportunities, opportunities to become better people, and opportunities to improve our decision-making and leadership skills. That is why I like the performance management system that employs a 360-degree approach so highly. It makes it possible for CEOs to get input from their workforce.

We must understand that the people we interact with on a daily basis—both at work and in our personal lives—are a constant source of learning opportunities, opportunities to become better people, and opportunities to improve our decision-making and leadership skills. That is why I like the performance management system that employs a 360-degree approach so highly. It makes it possible for CEOs to get input from their workforce. So, that's one method of mentoring a CEO. Because when you get criticism, all mentorship truly involves is someone holding up a mirror to you, pointing out your blind spots, and utilising their own expertise to help you improve. Because when you get criticism, what mentorship really involves is someone holding up a mirror to you, showing you where your blind spots are, and then utilising their own expertise to help you improve in the areas where you are challenged. Because human beings have both strengths and weaknesses, we must be willing to work on our flaws and reach out to those who can assist us in overcoming them in order to become a more complete person.

Even if you have a deep grasp of diversity and inclusion in a local setting, thinking about diversity in a global setting introduces several difficulties that have an impact on your diversity strategy. These difficulties revolve around two fundamental problems. You must first comprehend how other nations view diversity in order to manage diversity across national boundaries. This calls for an understanding of how a country's social, legal, and political landscape may affect how diversity and inclusion initiatives should be carried out there. Due to the stark contrasts across nations, multinational corporations should employ a multi-domestic strategy. Top organisations advise that you're going to need to make your diversity plan local, not just worldwide.

Let's discuss how to go about it. It goes without saying that your employees members must be aware of the national ideals. This entails selecting employees first from the host nation in order to grasp the subtleties of the local culture and creating a hiring strategy that is in line with it. In terms of the law, it is probable that you will need to modify your diversity strategy in some way while operating in another nation. So, how should this be accomplished? The creation of a neighbourhood diversity council is my top suggestion. The council should be well-versed in the customs and culture of the area.

Additionally, they might offer suggestions on how your business can adapt its approach to the particular region. The local diversity council could highlight how the selection criteria, the recruiting approach, or even the goals themselves would need to be modified to accommodate the local culture. I'll give you a simple illustration. Let's say you wish to strengthen parental leave regulations. The federal government of the United States provides 12 weeks of unpaid leave to its citizens. Twitter and American Express both provide five months. Four-month terms are offered by Deloitte, Ernst & Young, and Bank of America. Adoptions, inclusiveness of both genders and same-sex couples, and parental leave might all be viewed as components of these organisations' diversity strategies.

Imagine if they had now established a presence in Serbia. Mothers in Serbia receive a full year of paid leave, whereas fathers only receive one week. Therefore, adopting Etsy's six-month rule for any parent is absurd. Bank of America would have to raise its paid maternity leave to six months solely to comply with the legislation if it opened a branch in India.

Likewise, the Indian Supreme Court outlawed same-sex unions in 2013. In that location, exchanging a kiss with a person of the same sex carries a 10-year prison sentence. As a result, Bank of America's support for LGBTQ rights and their policy of granting parental leave to same-sex couples has generated considerable controversy. And that's only the legal aspect. When you consider a nation's social conventions, it gets much more challenging. In order to assist you navigate the challenging global waters, I thus advise you to hang on to your beliefs while thinking locally and taking into account a local diversity council. You must assess diversity because what is measured matters. However, you must first identify your objectives.

The CEOs of the top businesses, like Starbucks, Medtronic, and Intel, set explicit quantitative targets for diversity and hold employees accountable for achieving those goals. You ought to take this action as well. But you need some useful benchmarks before you can make goals. Many businesses claim to be able to quantify diversity, but how? So a US corporation may claim that 20% of its board is made up of women. Can they judge if something is good or bad and how? How do you establish objectives and targets for diversity? You may start by examining the population you are using as a sample. For instance, women make up 50% of the population in the US. Two, you may compare yourself to graduates of colleges. So, even if there are 50% of women in the US, how many women graduate as engineers? By the way, that's 20%. So perhaps you should dial that number. Third, you may look at industry norms and raise the bar. Only 11% of engineers in active practise are female. The fourth option is to observe what the top players in your sector are doing. 27% of Facebook's most recent engineering recruits were female.

Do these numbers make sense to use, though, if you're in Japan or Oman? No Only 5% of engineers in Japan are female. Furthermore, 53% of engineers in Oman are female. The point is that you must conduct the benchmarking in a culturally appropriate setting. When it comes to diversity, you must employ objectives and statistics if you want it to be effective. But in order to achieve that, you need some useful benchmarks.

We talked about improving inclusiveness and diversity in the current global context, and I appreciate you coming along on this trip with me. After completing this course, you need to have a organisation understanding of how to develop a diversity and inclusion plan and how you might wish to modify it to suit a particular local situation.

Alternately, decide to stick with a worldwide strategy for your whole organisation. You have a solid toolkit of strategies to improve hiring, lessen prejudice in selection, pick the finest team-specific training programme, and boost inclusiveness. Recall a few important lessons. To make sure diversity initiatives are successful, you must measure them just as you would anything else. To achieve this, you must first identify pertinent national goals and then figure out how to make sure that all of your efforts are held accountable.

You clearly understand the importance of diversity and inclusion, and now that you have some excellent tools at your disposal, you can use them to support your team as you continue on your own personal path.
There is more to variety than just the notion that it should occur spontaneously, which makes it challenging in China. We may discuss East Asia, like China, inside Asia, where collectivist principles are quite prominent. This makes the discussion of diversity challenging due to the significance of one's personal network.

One could object to the concept of expanding one's network in order to increase variety. In reality, nepotism, which is frowned upon in the US, is accepted as normal in

China. It would be immoral to refuse to employ a member of your family if that person needed a job. What is the actual situation with regard to diversity in China? The most significant efforts are being made to broaden gender diversity in China and much of Asia. With more than 50% of the labour force being female and around 36% of top managers being female, China is one of the most successful Asian nations in achieving gender diversity.

Despite this, there are still too few women on China's business boards. In China, where the population is mostly racial homogeneous, there is actually very little emphasis on fostering ethnic variety. Asia has poor LGBTQ rights as well, with Beijing, China being ranked as the least hospitable city in the world. What thus promotes variety in China? Although formal recruitment procedures are effective, just 50% of businesses now have them. As the number of women in leadership positions has nearly doubled across Asia, China may likewise think about expanding its leadership initiatives.

Businesses in China have a lot of room to expand, and as they do, their diversity and inclusion initiatives can change as well. The idea of Asia being a single region is a ridiculous idea. Asia is home to 60% of the world's 4.3 billion inhabitants. It is not surprising that China and India are two of the largest developing markets because they alone account for 37% of the world's population. Starting with India People in Asia often hold the view that variety will arise without any active effort being put in, and this is also true in India. Only 50% of businesses in Asia even have official diversity initiatives. India has fallen behind other countries in terms of employment diversity, and men and women in society usually experience extreme levels of inequality.

Women still want their husbands' approval before working. According to data on diversity in India, just 5% of corporate boards are made up of women. However, since the Business Act of 2013 obliged public companies to have at least one woman on their board, the percentage of women on corporate boards has increased. According to a KPMG poll, there hasn't been enough effort put into promoting diversity in India. To attain greater diversity, they advise, quote, "voluntary diversity objectives," "alignment between board composition and strategy," and "going beyond personal networks" when appointing directors. In India, likewise, trails behind in terms of sexual orientation, although in 2017, the Supreme Court upheld the right to privacy with regard to sexual orientation.

In India, people with disabilities are likewise not treated equally and are mostly excluded from the labour field. What thus promotes variety in India? Enterprises in India that formally promote diversity hire a third more women than non-diverse companies. Even more of an impact is made in these areas via mentoring and leadership programmes. Leadership initiatives that prioritised women nearly quadrupled the proportion of women in leadership positions in businesses across Asia. However, a study revealed that women in India had virtually no access to such programmes. Increasing leadership and mentoring programmes specifically geared at women would be a terrific idea since it is clear that mentoring has a significant influence on women in India, where there are five times as many women managers and twice as many women executives. We hope that equality will be attained in India, but there is still much work to be done.

How to gauge the performance of a diversity programme: It's crucial to make sure that once your diverse personnel are employed, they are not subjected to discrimination. This implies that men and women are paid equally and have equal access to advancement. According to my personal study, minorities and white people are treated quite differently at work than men and women. For instance, in order to be given consideration for a high-potential programme, women must do better than their male peers. People are astonished that there are so few women present since they genuinely need to do better. It seems obvious that you'll have more women if you don't set a higher bar for them to clear.

As another illustration, a study of US boards revealed that women needed much more experience than men did in order to be appointed to a Fortune 500 board. People claim that the lack of women on boards is due to their lack of experience. If you demand more experience from women than you do from men, this is true. When it comes to race, the statistics are considerably worse. In any case, what can your business do? My recommendations are fairly similar to those about choice. Before evaluating candidates, you should establish your criteria; this will increase the number of women and minorities who are hired.

Additionally, Goldman Sachs did something rather intriguing in terms of advertising. They contrast a list of candidates only based on merit. Therefore, if there is a mismatch between employees who are suggested for promotion by their superiors and those who are merely the best employees in terms of sales or customer happiness or anything else, they may check for bias. Inequity in compensation is, in my opinion, one of the biggest worldwide disparities. Of course, as Gap Inc. and Salesforce found, this is also the easiest to test for. Every organisation has to test for and then swiftly address any gender and racial wage discrepancies. Not only is this the proper thing to do, but it is also against the law in the US to pay anyone differently depending on their race or sex. Data is essential for examining salary disparities or other biases.

Even if you inform your boss or employees members that there is prejudice, their reactions may change significantly after they see it for themselves in the data. Then you must include more responsibility. include dashboards Make awards based on diversity measures. Inform the public about their successes and failures. You worked so hard to bring the greatest talent in, and you don't want to just lose them now. This is valid in a local setting, but it has even more significance when considered from a global perspective.

Companies are promoting diversity and inclusion in a variety of ways. Others place a stronger emphasis on inclusion, enabling people to bring their entire selves to work, while others place an emphasis on diversity, expanding the number of underrepresented groups. Let's discuss initiatives to promote diversity. Increasing the depth of recruitment efforts to obtain a more diversified talent pool is the simplest sell for a business. There is no indication that anyone is gaining an undue advantage from this.

However, if you examine your application statistics and discover that your candidate pool is not diverse, you may be able to make a difference by simply expanding your recruitment efforts. Consider this: how do you often learn about new positions? your system. If the majority of your organisation's employees are white men, then so will be the majority of their networks. In actuality, our networks resemble ourselves quite a bit. Therefore, we need to figure out how to connect with those who aren't generally part of our network. This can entail hiring from historically black universities or more diversely represented businesses. Not only would this boost diversity, but it would also raise the calibre of your candidate pool. If you just hire white guys from the 31% of the population in the US, for instance, you won't be getting the greatest talent available.

In fact, you're getting the top talent by enlarging your talent pool. You're making art. From the whole population, you are selecting the greatest individuals. Surprisingly, however, just 10% of international businesses claim to be making such an effort to increase their talent pool. Therefore, this could be an excellent solution for your business. The second thing that businesses frequently do is search for strategies to lessen prejudice throughout the hiring process. I'll give you an illustration of bias: Numerous studies have been carried out by experts in the US and Canada using real resumes submitted for real jobs. They are false resumes, and the applicant's sex or race is the only difference. They discover that a CV that is exactly the same except for the name to be that of a white male increases the likelihood of receiving a callback and increases the beginning wage. Our prejudices are powerful, and it may be quite challenging to get past them.

Therefore, removing all identifying information from resumes is one technique to eliminate the possibility of prejudice. Blinding the selecting process is what this is. According to research by the consulting organisation Gap Jumpers, when standard resume screening is used, 80% of candidates who advance to the first round of interviews are white, male, and physically fit individuals from prestigious colleges. Blind selection yielded a result of 40%. By establishing clear criteria before you analyse candidate applications or conduct interviews, you may also lessen prejudice. Google, which was renowned for its eccentric interview questions, has actually abandoned them in favour of more formal tests with clearly stated success criteria. Additionally, organisations like PWC, Facebook, Coca-Cola, and Lockheed-Martin provide training on unconscious bias to help individuals become aware of their prejudices. There are several approaches to boosting diversity. These are but a few of the ones that businesses utilise the most. increasing talent pool diversity and subsequently reducing prejudice in the hiring process.

There are several ways for businesses to step up their inclusion initiatives. Several businesses provide mentorship and coaching programmes to help ensure that women and minorities have an equal chance at success. For instance, the German corporation Siemens, which manufactures industrial equipment, has a programme called "Women and their path within the organisation". It employs coaching, mentoring, and training to assist women in achieving leadership positions. Such initiatives can improve the retention of bright women. In one of my own studies, I discovered that placing women in high-potential pools also reduced turnover—but only if they had other women in positions of authority above them, such as a female manager.

The research strongly suggests that having some women in high leadership positions inside a organisation is crucial for sending a message to other female employees that there are opportunities for progression. Another method to enhance inclusion is by eliminating a significant institutional prejudice that makes it harder for women to compete in the workforce. Someone's family. Companies like Colgate Palmolive include work-life initiatives into their talent strategy, such as flexible work schedules or condensed workweeks. To encourage work-life balance, they provide emergency in-home childcare for dependents and financial aid for tuition.

Thanks to all of these initiatives, women may now bring their whole selves to work. However, they're also helpful for drawing in and keeping millennials, who frequently desire more work freedom. Employer resource groups, or ERGs, are another feature common to most businesses. referred to as affinity groups. Diversity councils have replaced ERGs at other businesses, including Deloitte. All of these organisations exist to provide social assistance by facilitating connections between people who have common interests.

However, they frequently provide some kind of instrumental assistance as well. They might provide access to specialised mentorship or training programmes, a channel for the ERG to reach high leadership, or even a mechanism to have one's opinion heard.Using a varied, multidisciplinary, or cross-functional task force to address an organisational problem is one concept I particularly enjoy. Even while diversity isn't the main goal, these do really bring different individuals together and improve inclusion. Medtronic is one of my favourite brands. One of the biggest medical equipment organisations in the world is this one. The programme is known as "culture circles". Teams strive to resolve a problem within the organisation, and then they assemble for a large competition to determine the best solutions. These cultural circles are really engaging, as I can attest from my attendance. The cultural challenge for the most recent year was to boost productivity.

Today's executives frequently view leading diversity initiatives successfully as their greatest challenge, especially in light of the complexities of a global workforce. I would explore the advantages of diversity generally and offers suggestions for how businesses might promote inclusiveness and diversity in a variety of cultural settings. I will discuss how stressing diversity may benefit your company, how to develop a local or global plan, and provides a practical example so that you can understand what a global diversity strategy entails in action.

I will discuss using benchmarks to assess the success of your diversity initiatives and provides information on how to promote inclusion and diversity in various cultural contexts. In the twenty-first century, businesses must successfully manage personnel in a rapidly changing global economy and maximise diversity and inclusion. In this part of this chapter, I'll cover how to optimise diversity and inclusion in a global organisation as well as the overlap between these two extremely challenging problems. The issue of how to promote equality at work in order to improve organisational performance and the general state of the globe intrigues me.

In this part of this chapter, I'll walk you through the process of creating a more successful diversity and inclusion strategy and demonstrate the best practises for applying that strategy in various cultural situations. If you do this correctly, your business may achieve new heights in terms of employee engagement, productivity, and performance. Let's start as the world is changing every minute. Even some of the finest businesses in the world struggle with inclusion and diversity.

It is today's greatest corporate challenge. But it is possible to succeed if we treat diversity and inclusion like any other organisational endeavour. Furthermore, there isn't much debate left at this time that it should be done even though it can be done. Business needs diversity to thrive. According to the McKinsey Global Institute, achieving full gender parity for women may boost global production by more than 25%. By 2025, that will be 12 trillion dollars. This suggests that the economy would increase by 25% if women participated fully in it. Finally, variety fosters invention.

Diversity of thought not only expands your market and boosts sales, but it also spurs more innovation within your company. Diverse viewpoints inspire innovative ways of thinking. One study found that having more women in top management positions at the S&P 1500 over a 14-year period improved financial results by 42 million dollars in company value. And when women were in senior management, businesses that promoted innovation experienced the biggest financial advantages.

Companies with more diversity just perform better. When we consider diversity in leadership positions in businesses, the findings are much more compelling. Most likely because there is the largest imbalance there. So, certainly, it is difficult. But we can manage this. Each journey begins with the first step. And this is both your and my path.

I want to briefly discuss what I mean by diversity and inclusion, or DNI, before we begin discussing it from a global perspective. Actually, there are two distinct aspects to this. Increasing the number of underrepresented groups in your company is part of the diversity component. If you work in a mostly male industry, this may also apply to women and people of colour. It may be seniors, veterans, disabled people, or members of the LGBT community. There are two approaches to boosting the representation of a certain group, such as women. You have the power to both increase the number of women you recruit and decrease the number of women leaving your company.

Additionally, diversity does not imply that your workforce is entirely comprised of males in IT and females in HR. When there are just male instructors and only female personnel, diversity is not an issue. Integration is necessary to consider diversity. People of different backgrounds must feel included in order to contribute to the organisation with their true selves. Additionally, inclusion has two key elements. People must initially feel included and at home. The second element is distinctiveness. This implies that you not only provide individuals a place to fit in, but also give them the freedom to be their own original selves. Instead of encouraging people to conform to a certain culture, you appreciate and welcome the distinctions you notice in them.

Each year, businesses spend billions of dollars on diversity initiatives, but with surprisingly little success. Too frequently, diversity initiatives are predicated on the erroneous belief that a sincere discussion about "privilege" is all that is required. That is insufficient. We must stop praising the issue and start working to find a solution if we are to make any progress.

I have offered an insightful critique of the conversation that is now being had about various forms of diversity in heterogeneous organisations all over the world. Your organisation culture has to be infused with diversity, inclusion, belonging, and equality for employees to feel welcomed, be their best selves, and perform at their best. This can be done by following clear, doable actions. Access these useful tools and suggestions for improving diversity, inclusion, belonging, and equality (DIBE) in your organisation to avoid the flawed procedures and communication methods that prevent progress in so many other organisations.

In order for each employee to achieve their maximum capacity, diversity management is essential. Every employee is expected to perform satisfactorily, and managers want nothing less from them. However, diversity and its management are frequently not seen as direct factors in the effectiveness and financial health of the firm. Among all the various challenges that businesses face, managing and utilising diversity are frequently devalued since they are separated from the rest of the organization. Although there isn't a single, tried-and-true "solution" to diversity, and there isn't a simple way to handle implementation hurdles, this chapter aims to highlight current methods of promoting diversity's benefits while also paving the way for a broader understanding of its meanings.

"Organisations with a varied mix of genders are more likely to be profitable than average. We may draw the conclusion from the data point that diversity helps the organisation be more productive, efficient, and competitive as well as have a favourable effect on the bottom line."

- Dr. Amit Das

CHAPTER TWO

Nurturing Inclusion & Belonging In The Workplace For Greater Progress

"No matter who we are or what we look like or what we may believe, it is both possible and, more importantly, it becomes powerful to come together in common purpose and common effort." – Oprah Winfrey

Inclusion refers to our efforts to accept and appreciate the differences that make us unique and to create an inclusive and fair workplace where everyone has the chance to succeed at every important moment. We still haven't mastered that part, but if people consider the critical moments, I'm confident that inclusive behaviours will emerge. These behaviours include how we coach our leaders; how we lean in to recognise when a culture's additions don't fit; how we widen our horizons to accept differences; and how we search for the additions that are different. An inclusive organisation culture improves opportunities and morale. Millennials favour diverse employment environments. It often has lower rates of employees turnover, saving a lot of time and money on hiring processes. Employing a diverse workforce shows a organisation has good values and a solid reputation in the job market.

"Organisations with inclusive cultures are twice as likely to surpass financial goals. The likelihood of good performance increased by three times. Being inventive and agile is six times more probable. And eight times more likely to provide successful organisation results."

According to a PwC study, millennial women look for organisations that have a track record of valuing diversity; 85% employers feel this is crucial. Because having a diverse group of demographic traits alone won't affect an organisation's bottom line unless the members of each demographic feel included, inclusion must be viewed as significantly distinct from diversity. A sense of cultural and environmental inclusion is referred to as inclusion.

"The importance of diversity and inclusion in determining an organisation's culture cannot be overstated."

With digitalization and organisational advancement, the working culture of today has undergone a significant transformation. The benefits of having a diverse employees are apparent, and they are used to keep the finest personnel in the organisation. Diversity refers to a person's age, gender, educational background, cultural background, personality, beliefs, and much more, in addition to their nationality. And because diversity, inclusion, belonging and equality (DIBE) are so essential to creating a positive workplace culture, all shrewd businesses have adopted these concepts. Here are some examples of how DIBE influences how an organisation operates:

Despite being more challenging than managing a non-diversified organisation, managing a varied culture provides advantages. Organisations with a variety of cultures typically function substantially better. An organisation has additional and creative methods to contact their target audience with a employees like that. According to studies by McKinsey, businesses with a diverse culture have a higher likelihood of generating 21% more revenue than other businesses.

A smart organisation is defined as one that is knowledge-driven, internet-based, dynamically adaptive to new organisational forms and practises, agile in its ability to create and take advantage of opportunities presented by the new economy, and learning-driven.

According to the findings of another study, it's possible that traditional paradigms that put an excessive emphasis on profitability and efficiency won't be sufficient to comprehend the dynamics of the future multi-cultural organisation. A step in the right direction would be to place more emphasis on the present trend toward flat, decentralised, and nonhierarchical organisational structures. Above all else, though, is the development of a culture that appreciates and recognises the benefits and difficulties that come with having a diverse workforce.

Married women were perceived as sliding off the employment curve as juggling home and work without additional help became difficult, which was one of the primary causes of this gap. Finding the correct opportunity becomes difficult since women are frequently not viewed as being qualified for employment following a personal break, with maternity leaves being the main culprit. Organisations have worked to increase the number of women in the workforce for many years, but the outcomes are frequently confined to involvement at lower levels of the hierarchy. The proportion of women in top positions starts to decline as one climbs the hierarchical ladder.

The fact that there are more women working now than ever before shows that the emphasis has switched from quantity to quality, as well as whether or not female employees participate in decision-making and hold positions of authority and influence.

According to a 2019 UN Women report, despite international attempts to close the pay gap, there is still an inequity between men and women's incomes. And as a result of this difference, women often suffer more since they are forced to sacrifice their jobs in order to take on more duties for family care.

While the pandemic crisis continues to have a big influence on businesses and organisations, women are making progress in leadership recently, especially in top positions. Given the importance placed on balancing both personal and professional goals, women are performing roles that are substantially more complex than those played by men. Women are now stepping up and multitasking, pushing forward in their own industries despite these mounting demands and tiredness. By empowering their teams and promoting equality, diversity, and inclusion, women are becoming stronger leaders.

Many people continue to contest the reality of gender wage disparities. They continue to think that the deficit is just made up, notwithstanding the statistics. Thus, increasing awareness is the first step in closing the pay gap. Start a conversation about the salary gap with more people and the larger community. Encourage them to look more closely at the research on pay inequality research.

International Equal Pay Day is being observed as a reminder for us all to keep up the battle to abolish employee pay discrimination. The same survey revealed that female employees earn 23% less than male employees worldwide. Even worse, the pay for women of colour is just half that of white males. As more and more women retire into poverty, income disparity also persists, demonstrating the long history of pay discrimination against women.

Progressive actions have been taken throughout history to address the gender wage and inclusion gap. Sensitisation workshops for recruiters and hiring managers are held to promote campus diversity hiring, proactive safety solutions for women, career and professional development for women, women alumni rehiring, hyper-local targeted high-potential female leadership succession candidates, and increased representation of women in leadership roles. By encouraging male workers to promote gender diversity and inclusion, top management may successfully fuel a organisation's commitment to a culture of inclusive leadership.

What does the ideal workplace look like?

An advanced workplace is inclusive and diversified. Employees strive to work in workplaces that are supportive of innovation, employee friendliness, alignment, engagement, and focus on performance. This may be accomplished by making sure there is equality and diversity within the organisation. Many surveys show that between 70% to 80% of job seekers prioritise diversity and inclusion. Diverse and inclusive businesses are seen as bringing innovation and changing the sector with strategic consequences, in addition to being a coveted trait among potential workers. Leading experts claim that organisations with a diversity of racial and ethnic backgrounds are more likely to achieve financial returns of 30% to 40% higher than the matching national industry medians.

The organisation's inclusive and varied work culture should be represented by its employees, who should be its diversity ambassadors. Organisations now frequently work with teams that are dispersed around the globe. It is critical to make ongoing efforts to generate a variety of opportunities that support and build a diverse global workforce. Supporting international clients by bridging cultural, political, and economic divides will allow the organisation to train employees and executives to become diversity synergists, both within the organisation and with customers.

In order to ensure diversity inside the organisation, equality of opportunity is essential. Leading positions in business are determined by traits like attention to detail, tenacity, enthusiasm, dedication, community building, and long-term strategic vision rather than factors like gender, religion, socioeconomic standing, etc. The organisation's professional development should ultimately be driven by merit, with career progression solely dependent on a person's attitude, qualifications, performance, and ability.

Bias-free hiring practises should be followed at all levels. Despite their physical limitations, gender, or ethnicity, they are well-qualified regardless of the position you intend to fill and the department. In the end, a person's contributions are what allow a business to advance to the next stage. Organisations should examine their present hiring practises to identify any obstacles to achieving diversity.

The organisations should carefully and correctly explain the corporate policies to all of their employees. Any non-compliance can be brought up with the CEO or the HR department. The need for reviewing practises and policies involving diversity promotion for appropriateness and relevance at least once a year cannot be overstated.

Organisations must be encouraging and inclusive in order to encourage everyone to excel in their current role and advance into leadership positions. Organisations with inclusive cultures will be better positioned to address future issues in a world that is continually developing. In order to secure the expansion of the economy, it is essential to make significant decisions from a balanced viewpoint. Truly diverse and inclusive workplace cultures can only be created as a consequence of the steadfast efforts made by numerous organisational stakeholders.

Employers who offer equal opportunity tend to attract more employees. They have access to a range of resources and are more knowledgeable and conscious of their surroundings. Women at work should be given the chance to return, allowing them to rejoin the job after taking a little break. A very beneficial enabler is extending office diversity to guaranteeing equitable physical access within the workplace. Increased involvement and engagement among employees members and the larger community may be achieved by reducing access obstacles such as those based on sexual orientation.

According to a Boston Consulting Group (BCG) study, people who report being pleased at work are 1.5 times more likely to claim that they always desire to provide their best effort. This emphasises the connection between inclusion and innovation and workplace pleasure. Diversity and inclusion must be knitted into the fundamental fabric of organisations, something that must be actively pursued by those organisations. For instance, at Ericsson, diversity and inclusion have been central to our culture and core principles.

We cultivate it in all that we do, forming teams that represent our strategy and providing a forum for all workers to share their own viewpoints. We must do this for the benefit of our customers, employees, and society as a whole. In fact, we organisationly believe that inclusive, varied teams not only foster performance and creativity but also increase the value of the organisation.

Flex is the skill of moving between leadership philosophies to more successfully interact with those who think differently than you. You're very different from you in terms of generation, culture, and gender. It's about adjusting to the individuals across from you in order to get the greatest outcomes, not fundamentally altering who you are and expanding your leadership style.

The workforce is changing and has been changing for a while. I estimate that 36% of the workforce is made up of multicultural individuals. There are a lot of demographic changes affecting our workforce, including the fact that women make up nearly half of the labour force. I believe they account for 70% of purchasing decisions, and millennials are becoming a larger portion of the labour force.

However, I'm not sure if managers always know how to work with this new workforce or how to better engage and motivate these new workers who are entering the workforce. Additionally, there is a price to not flexing. For instance, I believe the Gallup survey from last year estimated that disengaged employees cost the world between $450 and $550 billion. For these and other reasons, I believe there is a business case and an opportunity for the organisation to create a value proposition for their employees if they can do this properly.

You might have hired employees who may have one foot out the door, who really don't feel motivated and engaged, and who don't feel like the organisation is really speaking to them. The power gap is a very important aspect of the art of flexing. A power gap can be little or vast, depending on how much social distance there is between you and those in positions of authority. If you're the manager, the power gap also includes the distance between you and your team members.

What is the importance of creating an inclusive culture at work?

The leaving employee brought the best skill set for the role and had just been employed for six months. They earned a significant pay raise from their prior position, and nobody had observed any indications of unhappiness. After some reluctance, they responded, "I don't feel like I belong here, and I don't think anyone truly knows who I am," when asked why they were leaving at the departure interview.

Businesses that have been successful in building a diverse employees might benefit from the many viewpoints and experiences that come with it. However, seemingly harmless activities that are ingrained in a organisation's culture run the risk of alienating and alienating a portion of its workers. However, when the potential issues with these behaviours are detected, a dedication to fostering an inclusive culture can result in improvements that can significantly enhance a job.

As is clear, organisations concur that it is necessary to have specific strategies and a focal point for converting the DIBE vision into actions. However, before they can expect managers to expedite this process, they must first make sure that managers themselves support inclusiveness and don't only meet prescribed objectives.

We live in a varied world, and we want our workplace to reflect that. However, if we're going to improve and support diversity, we need inclusion strategies that foster and maintain a sense of equality and belonging. Inclusion is being asked to dance if diversity is being invited to the party. It will be necessary to cultivate an inclusive attitude that not only values diversity but also spots the instances where prejudice and preconceptions are negatively affecting your organisation's culture.

The activity of promoting fairness is the inclusion component, hopefully. It is the action of inviting you to the dance; it is the action of employing and attempting to implement ethical workplace procedures. That is inclusion, but the power of DIBEs can only be unlocked—and I mean this—when you have a genuine feeling of community in your heart and are free to be wholly yourself. And the impulse to belong is human—it is ingrained in each and every one of us genetically.

Your organisation's entire financial line will benefit as you raise employee satisfaction and retention rates. Let's make inclusion work for you. There are resources available to any organisation that may be used to implement a diversity and inclusion programme. Let's consider your resources and how you can use them. An asset is anything valued or helpful.

Everyone gains when women engage in the economy, the achievement of equal job opportunities, increased social justice, as well as national and international economic goals, depends on women's leadership and career equality.

Every organisation has extremely carefully thought-out diversity, equality, and inclusion policies that express the aims and activities in explicit terms. There is still a long way to go, but these policies have raised awareness and addressed a number of issues. To keep making progress toward gender equality and make it faster, we must all cooperate. Even the most well-intentioned activities become tactical and lose effect when gender imbalance is only seen as an issue to be solved by organising mentoring programmes for women or pushing promotions to the next level.

India is a varied nation, and the majority of employees at organisations come from various backgrounds to work as a team. Recently, and appropriately so, the topics of diversity and inclusion at work have come up in India, helped along by increased awareness on a global scale, social media conversation, regulatory measures, and forward-thinking business actions.

According to sources, women made up just 19.9% of the whole Indian labour force as per the National Family Health Survey 2019–21. These figures accurately represent the gender disparity that exists in Indian workplaces.

Women are frequently left feeling conflicted and unmotivated by the talk surrounding the extraordinary focus on women and the various interventions and policy changes to ensure women can succeed, because there is a chance that it will be interpreted as a requirement for greater skill and competency to achieve the same level of success as men.

In order to establish an atmosphere where women can participate on an equal basis, realise their full potential, and get full recognition and rewards without inciting resentment in males, we must fundamentally rethink and assess our programmes and initiatives. so that we don't run the danger of creating a brand-new kind of prejudice.

A basic human need that is encoded into our DNA is the yearning for social belonging. Nevertheless, 40% of workers report feeling lonely at work, which has led to poorer organisational commitment and engagement. In a nutshell, businesses are wasting money. Businesses in the United States spend close to $8 billion annually on diversity, inclusion, belonging, and equality (DIBE) training programmes that fall short because they ignore the need for us to feel included.

Do your employees feel like full-fledged members of the workplace?

If not, you need to improve your diversity, inclusion, belonging, and equality (DIBE) activities. Here are three things HR can do. All workers like to have a sense of community at work.

- To create a feeling of community, get rid of alienation, include everyone, and show that you care through rewards and projects.
- The majority of businesses actively aim toward having a diverse workforce, but many now also endeavour to make sure that all workers feel welcome there. HR executives have a fantastic chance to reassess their inclusion approach and goals through fostering a sense of belonging or an employee's idea of acceptance within a particular group.

The foundation of inclusion is a sense of belonging. When employees feel fully included, they believe the organisation values them as people—their true selves. HR plays a role in making things happen. It benefits workers and, in the end, boosts corporate success. According to Gartner research, organisations with sustained DIBE programmes exhibit a 20% boost in inclusion, which is correlated with higher on-the-job effort, a stronger desire to stick around, and good employee performance. Employees must feel like they belong to the organisation for them to have a feeling of belonging. Follow these three actions to foster a culture of belonging and accomplish DIBE objectives.

- Despite advancements in DIBE, many workers still experience exclusion at work, which leads them to further repress the aspects of who they are that set them apart from their coworkers. Being made to feel unwelcome is a psychologically upsetting and detrimental experience that interferes with concentration and performance. There shouldn't be a "one size fits all" workplace. However, the majority are still "one size fits some", with the assumption that everyone else would cram in.
- Cultures of belonging may be created quite effectively by initiatives like encouraging diversity in succession planning and hosting events to highlight underrepresented groups.
- Providing rewards and programmes that recognise individuals' distinctive contributions to the organisation proves that corporate performance is strongly related to how satisfied people are with their work.
- Benefits that are available to all demographic groups, such as flexible work hours and mental wellness initiatives, show workers that you are concerned about their individual requirements both at work and outside of it.

What does it mean when someone says they feel like they "belong" at work?

An organisation's sense of belonging is based on certain factors, according to research:

- Being recognised for your individual contributions.
- Feeling connected to your coworkers.
- Receiving support for your daily tasks and career advancement.
- Being proud of the goals and values of your organisation.
- By focusing on worker behaviour and assisting you in identifying and eliminating bias within procedures, you can help youself rewrite the playbook and ensure equal hiring, compensation, evaluations, and the assignment of promotable tasks.

Being a part of something doesn't always entail being liked by coworkers or feeling linked to your coworkers because you went to the same schools or live in the same areas.

What can organisation executives do to foster a sense of community at work?

According to the study, those who have a strong sense of "high belonging" at their workplace are more motivated and committed to their jobs, and they want to work there for at least two years. People who felt "poor belonging" were four times more likely to think that their occupations were stagnant.

According to the research data, there are multiple steps that organisations, senior leaders, managers, and peers may take to create and promote a culture of belonging at work. Here is a short summary of what each level needs to prioritise:

- Senior executives establish the tone for a organisation by embodying the principles of the organisation. Exemplifying inclusive leadership by paying attention to all team members' opinions and expressing openness towards their values, attempting to establish contact with workers around the organisation relating to personal experiences. The expectations of senior leadership are comparable to those described in earlier research in many aspects.

According to a survey, six out of ten people want to work for a organisation that shares their values and viewpoints. In addition, leadership is required to deliver on current challenges, including sustainability, retraining, diversity, and inclusion in the workplace. Employees feel supported, seen, and linked to their employment more when leadership shows a commitment to these concerns and is prepared to fight the good fight. The research data emphasises the importance of advancing factors that enable workers to be recognised and encouraged, such as fostering diverse leadership and incorporating DIBE into projects like employee succession planning.

- Managers uphold the culture through praising the efforts of their employees. Giving employees regular, frank feedback helps them do their jobs better. By addressing issues raised by employees recognising their workers' efforts in public that enable team members to take the initiative.

It's frequently said that people making the shift into management jobs become the kinds of supervisors they would have enjoyed working with as employees or team members. As a result, a fascinating overlap exists between elevating belonging at the management and employees levels. Team members and managers alike should be able to provide criticism and praise, as well as demonstrate responsiveness in their various responsibilities.

You can conclude by taking a closer look at how employees foster a sense of belonging among one another and, ultimately, create an inclusive culture. They respect the obligations of their coworkers outside of the workplace. You must give your coworkers honest, timely feedback on their job. Reward your coworkers' efforts. Show your gratitude for the efforts. You must discuss the working relationship with coworkers in an honest and open manner. For someone to feel noticed, connected, supportive, and proud, they must feel gratitude as well as respect for and support of one another's work-life balance.

Having a sense of belonging at work may improve everyone's productivity and work environment. But if it isn't already ingrained in the culture of your business, cultivating a sense of belonging can be challenging. People from different backgrounds should be given a seat at the table and should feel heard, visible, and appreciated for their contributions in order to foster a sense of belonging in the workplace. Employees can benefit from feeling like they belong at work, and 34% of individuals say that this is where they feel most at home. As teams began working remotely in 2020, the importance of belonging increased. According to research, during COVID-19, the importance of belonging increased by 12%. While fostering a sense of belonging is a vital aspect of organisational culture, it's equally crucial that each of us continuously build and refine our own sense of belonging.

Why is creating a sense of belonging important?

The loneliness of feeling like you don't belong may be crippling when you're working in a team. However, when you feel comfortable being yourself at work, you may put less emphasis on your interactions with your coworkers and more emphasis on the task at hand. Your confidence and persistence may increase if you feel like a member of the team, which will ultimately improve your performance.

Developing your own sense of community at work is advantageous to everyone. You're more inclined to be that ally for someone else when you feel like you belong. Being a strong leader at work involves growing your sense of belonging. Despite the fact that many businesses give diversity programmes top priority, many don't do enough to encourage belonging.

Fundamentally, the feeling of belonging is when someone feels included and accepted for who they truly are. Simply concentrating on diversity and inclusion is insufficient to maintain team members' interest. Many times, content workers also need to feel like they belong at work. Many businesses overlook inclusion and equity as crucial components when creating belonging initiatives. Organisations can fail to recognise the value of belonging.

Organisations that make a commitment to cultivating a sense of belonging among their employees also profit. According to a Gallup study, businesses with engaged workers are 22% more successful. It pays to promote belonging in your corporate culture since it plays a crucial role in employee engagement.

Even though you now feel excluded, acceptance of others and open-mindedness might make you feel included.

If you feel like your suggestions are consistently ignored, think about how the dialogue seems from other people's viewpoints. Was your attitude one of acceptance and receptivity? When you consider things from another person's perspective, it could be simpler to communicate your views.

Making inner work a priority might help you identify ingrained notions that make you feel different from other people. You can develop new beliefs via inner work that might foster a sense of belonging. You may identify what causes you to feel as though you don't belong by taking the time to focus on your inner self, both at work and at home.

According to a research data, belonging is evaluated on a 10-point scale based on the following factors:

- When you are seen at work, your coworkers acknowledge, appreciate, and respect you.
- Having pleasant, genuine social connections with coworkers, supervisors, and senior leaders at work is a sign that you are connected.
- When you have support at work from others around you, you are able to complete your tasks and lead a fulfilling life. These individuals might be senior leaders and peers.
- Being proud of your job and your organisation makes you feel in line with its goals, objectives, and core values.

Even if you don't currently feel like a member of the group, there are many ways to encourage a sense of teamwork at work. You don't need to wait long to start feeling like a valued team member if you're feeling lonely and like you don't belong at work. There are several ways you may increase your feeling of identity.

Our self-criticism frequently leaves a vacuum between us and our team. Self-isolation brought on by feeling inadequate may make collaboration very challenging. Integrating into the group might be made simpler by unconditional acceptance of who you are. Begin making efforts to promote a sense of belonging in other contexts, such as your family, neighbourhood, or spiritual community. When you feel at home and accepted in one social group, you become far more receptive to belonging in other social groups.

Consider how you fit in everywhere. If we feel excluded at work, we could also experience this feeling elsewhere in our lives. Make an effort to fit in. When we feel alone, we can pass up chances to build a feeling of community. Make a deliberate effort to try to belong while remaining true to who you are. You could feel more welcomed and included if you reached out to a coworker or participated in a team activity. Even better, urge your team to organise a bonding activity.

When you feel like the odd one out at work, it can be difficult to feel like you belong. But is that emotion new to you, or have you experienced it before? It's possible that you've formed self-limiting assumptions that make you feel alien. Understanding your own self-perceptions may be accomplished through evaluating your ideas. Uncertain about where to begin? To get you started, here are a few books on personal development.

Everyone wants to belong to something greater than themselves and feel welcomed, included, heard, and accepted. It's an essential human need that we value just as highly as food and shelter.

"A sincere relationship not only satisfies your employee's fundamental desire for inclusion and acceptance, but it also motivates them to work harder and boosts productivity."

But how can you foster and promote this sense of community inside your organisation? In light of the current situation, it is a very important question. It's hardly surprising that there is a sense of detachment given the large number of workers who are now working remotely and away from the office's social core. 20% of remote workers, according to a Forbes study, reported feeling a lack of a sense of belonging during the epidemic.

Employees are less likely to feel excluded from initiatives when they believe they have advocates who are dedicated to their inclusion. A team might feel like it belongs if even one ally leads in an equitable and inclusive manner. Belonging encourages group cooperation and, even though it lowers their personal performance, workers are less motivated to collaborate with their team when they feel excluded. Employees are far more inclined to share ideas and cooperate when they feel like they belong, meanwhile. Being a part of a team at work may increase inspiration, understanding, and trust. Having the impression that someone is on your side is usually beneficial.

Everyone wants to belong to something greater than themselves and feel welcomed, included, heard, and accepted. It's an essential human need that we value just as highly as food and shelter. In all facets of life, including our place of employment, it is crucial to feel appreciated as people and recognised for our accomplishments. The need to fit in is more intense in this situation. Based on how our coworkers and employer view us, we assess our value in relation to others and ourselves.

"Employees who have a strong feeling of connection are more motivated to perform well in their positions."

A sincere relationship not only satisfies your employee's fundamental desire for inclusion and acceptance, but it also motivates them to work harder and boosts productivity. But how can you foster and promote this sense of community inside your organisation? In light of the current situation, it is a very important question. It's hardly surprising that there is a sense of detachment given the large number of workers who are now working remotely and away from the office's social core.

The workplace of today is hybrid by nature. Hybridity need not negatively impact culture or leadership, despite the worries of many HR leaders. Accepting hybrids as a constant aspect of the contemporary workplace actually gives organisations the chance to modernise how they handle two crucial areas: altering culture and empowering leaders. In comparison to other talent priorities, DIBE is the one where 64% of CHROs claim their CEOs are most directly involved. You may examine the effectiveness with which inclusive behaviours are displayed within your team by using this self-assessment tool on inclusion.

A strong organisation serves as the cornerstone for a high belonging score. Senior leaders exist who can serve as examples. Senior leaders and employees have a number of similarities. Regardless of seniority or achievement, there is accountability for breaking business rules. There are transparent and reliable channels in place to report infractions of corporate policy.

Perhaps you've already realised that your employee has to be addressed with respect to this issue. All organisations need to embrace this inclusive culture. Organisations need employees that bring excitement, a feeling of emotional investment, and a dedication to going above and beyond just doing their daily tasks. Productivity rises when workers are highly engaged and motivated.

As vital to an employee as compensation, location, and perks are their levels of involvement. The ability to connect with a group, a leader, a brand, and an organisation is crucial to one's welfare and has an impact on their productivity at work. Belonging and engagement go hand in hand. Ambitious workers are aware that accomplishing their professional objectives will also result in them receiving personal incentives, such as promotions, commissions, or perhaps a new corner office. These are employees that believe that working is about more than just doing the job.

Creating a sense of belonging at work enhances employee satisfaction and a organisation's overall efficiency. Employee engagement requires belonging, which is a crucial element. When someone feels excluded, they frequently withdraw from their team and their task. Your organisation may change when you prioritise belonging in your culture. Employees who have a strong feeling of connection to the organisation are more likely to perform well in their positions. It is one of the main forces for increased worker involvement.

Here is a quick test to determine if you are addressing the problem. How frequently does your organisation handle each of the efforts for employee engagement listed below? Lack of activity in these areas is a warning sign of problems with employee engagement, or more particularly, it is a sign that a workforce may be disengaged.

- Do you plan to send out updates and news alerts frequently? Or perhaps you only communicate when there is a significant development to report? Maintaining frequent and consistent communication is crucial to prevent workers, particularly those who work from home, from developing a sense of alienation.
- You could be surprised by the outcomes if you let employees submit their own suggestions. Your employees not only have a wide range of unique perspectives to share, but if they have a voice in the process, they will be much more involved in the outcome. The process of ideas from conception to execution may be managed with the aid of an employee engagement app.
- Do you allow your remote employees to collaborate with their coworkers? Or do they operate independently? The finest teams are those that are freely collaborating and working towards a single objective. One of the biggest obstacles to employee engagement caused by the epidemic has been this feeling of isolation.
- The key to a successful recognition programme is to make sure that praise is delivered freely and in front of everyone. Workers will be inspired to work harder when they witness other people's accomplishments being recognised. One of the essential best practises for employee engagement is public acknowledgment.
- In a similar vein, employees who work from home suffer from a lack of opportunities for social interaction outside of the office. You may recreate the "water cooler" effect by setting up social platforms where employees can interact informally. The online social areas you create will boost employee engagement right away.

- Employee voice is a key idea and the foundation of fostering a sense of belonging. You may give employees the crucial feeling of being heard by providing a two-way communication channel. If you don't plan regular feedback opportunities, employees could feel ignored and silenced.

- Employers anticipate that their employees will accomplish their job objectives for the organisation as a whole as well as for themselves. But how can you start this at your organisation, especially when so many of your workers work remotely and are geographically distant?

- How can you naturally bind your remote employees together? Setting up corporate events is a fantastic way to promote genuine interaction and involvement. Even if current times may have prevented real events, you can nonetheless plan online get-togethers for your team. Regular events—virtual or not—should be your top goal for whatever technique you use to increase employee engagement.

- Too many businesses fail to inform their employees of the wider picture. They'll keep them informed about news that is pertinent to their work position but not about the organisation's general strategy and direction. This is incorrect. Employeess won't be very engaged at work until they understand their position within the organisation.

Even if the terminology has changed to include topics like "employees engagement" and "brand culture," the overarching objective of connecting all of your employees and incorporating everyone remains the same. The way we operate has changed drastically in response to recent developments in the business climate. These include the adoption of remote working, the use of online meetings, the development of employee engagement tools, and other innovations that enable businesses to electronically communicate with their workforces. The overall objective has not altered, notwithstanding the environment.

It may have an impact on the income and commercial objectives of your organisation, but it all begins at the top. The management group must take the initiative in creating a supportive environment and culture. Making employees feel like more than simply a paycheck number is what belonging is all about. Business executives must create a setting where employeess may interact, communicate, and be treated fairly. This is especially important for remote workers who could otherwise feel lonely and disengaged from the workplace community. Sharing your organisation's goals, beliefs, and future plans will help you enhance employee engagement by providing workers a clearer understanding of what the organisation wants to accomplish for them.

Giving your employees that crucial sense of belonging entails more than just making sure they are content and happy at work. They must be respected, heard, and acknowledged. People won't want to stay with your business if they don't feel like they belong there. They will ultimately experience pain and a sensation that something is always lacking. This may develop into a conviction that they are not respected, acknowledged, listened to, or a member of the organisation and its community.

Giving employees the whole picture adds value to them; people need to understand "the why" behind what they are doing. An organisation's ability to convey its brand values, aims, and future goals offers its employees motivation and a clear understanding of how their individual actions affect the business as a whole. The greatest place to begin when looking into employee engagement is by providing a "why" response.

How to transform employees into valuable colleagues rather than mindless cogs in the system?

Employees at a strong organisation feel like they are a part of something bigger than themselves. They don't experience assimilation or conformity pressure, or exclusion or rejection because of who they are. They perceive themselves as insiders and are honoured for their distinctive contributions.

When conducting private employee surveys, Great Place to Work gathers information about management, promotion procedures, emotional and psychological safety, and other topics. These ratings show whether employees feel like they fit in or like outsiders. High-belonging workplaces routinely produce superior financial returns. According to the study, 64% of employees are more inclined to participate in intense innovation when they believe they "make a difference."

Backstabbing and office politics can erode trust and give employees the impression that their employment isn't really fair. Competitive cultures can harm community and camaraderie, yet competition itself can be good. As a result of "executive blinders," a phenomenon where males in executive roles are 2.6 times more likely than female executives at the same organisation to perceive equal treatment for all employees, poor leadership can also create blind spots.

Even executives who are dedicated to fostering an egalitarian workplace must push themselves to identify their shortcomings. While 52% of ERG leaders concur,

100% of executive sponsors of employee resource groups claim that organisation leadership promotes involvement among ERGs. The creation of an inclusive workplace will be hampered by poor leadership and partiality, but under strong leadership, everyone will feel at home.

Make knowledge available in an equitable and open manner. Despite the fact that the statistics clearly demonstrate that organisations that prioritise their mission are more likely to have happy employees, this information is meaningless without effective communication. Siloed communication makes it harder to work together and be a team. Some employees get the message that they are outsiders who shouldn't be trusted with sensitive corporate secrets. They may feel cheated and misled if they are caught off guard by negative news or kept in the dark about important organisation choices. Everyone in the organisation benefits from open, cross-team communication because it makes them feel important.

By praising employees for their efforts, a organisation conveys how much it respects each individual's potential. Employees who feel valued are more likely to say that they are cared for by their employer and that their team is more cohesive. Programs for recognition also assist with other aspects of belonging. People who feel constantly acknowledged at work fare better than those who do not.

According to the research, organisations that are able to embrace new team members (and their ideas) do better than their rivals. Consider the effect of a new team member. What skills or knowledge do they offer that you are eager to discuss? Don't link all employee benefits to job tenure. New employees will feel excluded if they are unable to fully experience the workplace. Start involving them in crucial organisation tasks right away. For corporate executives, the idea of fostering a sense of welcome is not alien. It's frequently done for consumers and clients, and employees may apply these values with ease. It only requires dedication.

Employees must feel like they can bring their complete selves to work in order to build a sense of belonging. Many people don't feel secure doing it in their existing workplace. In comparison to the average workplace, 88% of employees at the Fortune 100 Best Organisations to Work For® are free to be themselves. Make sure you find methods to appreciate diversity so that workers feel free to be their whole, authentic selves. Make sure your business is comfortable "talking gay" and bringing attention to the experience of LGBTQIA+ employees and their allies. By working with ERGs, you can celebrate cultures and customs that are significant to your employees.

Be open-minded to other people's job experiences if they differ from your own. Make sure to do a employees survey and look at any areas where your business is lagging. The CEO and frontline employees alike must be committed to cultivating a sense of belonging for the whole organisation. As employees continue to reevaluate their relationship to work and what they expect from an employer, the greatest workplaces will give it top attention.

- Are you interested in the opinions of your employees regarding your business?
- Are you still attempting to solve the nuanced problem of employee engagement in your organisation?
- Have you been successful in gaining the real business advantages of high employee engagement?

Find out how to evaluate your performance and how to change the culture at your place of employment. According to Forbes, organisations with strong employee engagement may increase their profitability by 21%. That does really sound incredible. It is also true, though, that not all organisations have been successful in fostering the type of involvement that may significantly boost their ability to succeed in the marketplace. Measure the level of belonging, equity, inclusion, and diversity in your workplace. To back up this claim, Gallup estimates that just 36% of US workers are actively working. This explains why businesses are now eager to examine certain cutting-edge and distinctive engagement-boosting tactics.

However, by fostering a strong sense of workplace belonging in your employeess, you can assist you in achieving above-average levels of employee engagement. Employees experience a variety of emotions at work that are a reflection of their dedication, conduct, and confidence. As a leader, you must evaluate their sense of belonging to their organisation among all of these sensations and emotions.

"Workplace belongingness, put simply, refers to how appreciated and accepted your workers feel at work."

Employees that have a strong feeling of belonging demonstrate the conviction that they belong at work and are important to the organisation. In addition, their level of emotional attachment to their employers and organisations is influenced by their sense of belonging. Simply put, your employees will be more loyal if they experience a strong feeling of belonging. Additionally, they will learn how their personal achievements are related to organisational development.

"A strong feeling of belonging improves performance and self-assurance. In truth, the confidence that your organisation exudes is reflected in the self-assurance and morale of your employees."

The several ways that workplace belonging may increase employee engagement are explained in the section that follows. Let's discuss the ramifications of workplace belonging now that we all agree on what it means to organisational growth.

- Performance levels will inevitably rise once you are successful in instilling that degree of confidence in them. Can you do it incredibly effectively despite your lack of confidence in yourself? To be truthful, the possibilities are undoubtedly quite slim. Having said that, in order to direct your employees' confidence in the proper direction, you must encourage a stronger sense of belonging in them. The basic idea is that performance and confidence work best together. When workers feel appreciated, they will constantly be driven to do better and contribute more to the organisation.

- An accurate and reliable indicator of effective workforce management, engagement, and satisfaction is absenteeism. When seen from a larger perspective, there may be a variety of individualised causes for excessive absenteeism in a workplace. Among these causes, a lack of a sense of community at work is undoubtedly important. To put it another way, workers will only have the desire to go to a place of employment if they have a strong feeling of affiliation and belonging. The more engagement there is in your organisation, the lower the absence rate will be. Create a workplace that people want to be a part of every day. Give your employees an environment that encourages their best efforts each and every day.

- According to the Harvard Business Review, there is a clear link between employee engagement and trust. The following observations provide an explanation for this association. Employee engagement is 76% greater and productivity is 50% higher in high-trust organisations. Employee energy levels increase by 106% when trust is ingrained in the corporate culture as a natural virtue.

- This increases the workforce's resilience. The ability to be resilient has incalculable value in today's corporate environment. Difficult problems like the COVID-19 outbreak in recent years have put businesses to the test. While some businesses failed, some that were adaptable enough to these changes thrived. The ability to be resilient is now highly valued in the workplace. It directly supports involvement as well. Employees that possess resilience maintain their positive attitude in the face of difficult situations.

To support this, Deloitte research shows that having a strong sense of belonging at work may boost employees' job performance by 56%. The reaserach data also emphasises how a sense of belonging at work may reduce employee turnover by 50%. Clearly, the secret of job motivation is in a sense of belonging. Do you realise that? You must now take action to improve the engagement situation for your organisation.

Otherwise, they have a variety of justifications from which to choose for missing work. Additionally, they will be better able to grasp their obligations if they feel strongly like they belong. As a result, they won't depart on a whim to prolong the situation. In addition, it has been demonstrated that workplace belonging and absenteeism are mutually exclusive. According to research, businesses may cut the number of sick days used by employees by 75% by encouraging a strong feeling of workplace belonging. To do this, it is crucial to cultivate among employees strong sentiments of belongingness that allow them to engage more actively.

Employee satisfaction rises by 29% in trust-building organisations. Burnout rates are 40% lower and stress levels are 76% lower in workplaces where coworkers have high trust in one another. It is surprising how a single quality of trust can propel a organisation to extraordinary heights. We must ascertain the relationship between trust and belonging at work. The foundation of trust is acceptance, and this will always be true.

Employees are more inclined to trust their coworkers when they feel welcomed, respected, and appreciated. This is how the importance of belongingness for healthy working relationships that can promote high engagement is demonstrated. People that have high levels of trust work together more effectively and lead their organisations to new heights of achievement. Are you prepared to go above and beyond to build a strong sense of trust in your business? You need to set an example as a leader.

Among the most important trends in the modern workplace are inclusion and diversity. More than ever, businesses are keen to embrace the benefits of inclusion and diversity in the workplace. Hiring a diverse employees might not be enough for that, though.

You must make inclusion a core value of your business culture if you want to get the most out of your diverse team. This is where fostering a strong feeling of workplace community among your employeess may be really beneficial. When you encourage your workers to have a strong sense of belonging at work, you also provide them with the opportunity to participate in decision-making and express their opinions. Or, to put it another way, when employees feel like they belong, they feel more inclined to contribute. They provide original concepts and insightful observations that may be very beneficial to any business in their eagerness to increase the organisation's worth.

In order to maintain your competitive advantages in today's fiercely competitive business environment, you must innovate at every level. What could be better than a team that is eager to provide fresh, original ideas each day? An employee that doesn't hesitate to take initiative might really be quite valuable. You may encourage more creative freedom in your employees by encouraging a stronger sense of belonging among them. This creative freedom will serve as the cornerstone for a significant increase in employee engagement.

Overall, cultivating a sense of belonging among your employees may increase inclusivity in a variety of ways. Additionally, this greater diversity will boost workplace participation in a variety of ways.

As a manager, you would always want your employees to demonstrate excellent resilience. But how can employers encourage people to be resilient? When there is a strong sense of belonging, employees will give their all to support their organisations. If they aren't certain that they are a worthwhile contribution to the organisation, why would they want to take on so many tasks for their organisations? Therefore, it is true to state that by encouraging a sense of belonging among your employees, you may increase their resilience and, as a result, engagement.

To summarise, fostering a strong sense of workplace belonging among employees has a number of positive effects. When you assist your employees in developing a stronger bond with your business, they will feel appreciated and empowered to perform at their very best. It seems considerably more crucial to focus on encouraging a sense of belonging among employees, particularly when it comes to a diverse workforce. The secret to achieving high employee engagement is in your capacity as a leader to foster a sense of belonging among your team members.

Businesses and CEOs across sectors have committed to being more inclusive and diverse as they recognise the importance of including people with disabilities as well as diversity in racial, gender, and cultural backgrounds. The Great Resignation, a tide of individuals quitting their employment willingly, is still going strong. The COVID-19 pandemic-related worldwide event, which began in early 2021, significantly altered the workplace. Employees rank purpose-driven work as a top priority, along with greater pay, better benefits, more opportunity for growth, and work-life balance. And their superiors are closely watching.

However, do women actually have equal opportunities?

Women have repeatedly complained about being regarded incompetently and experiencing gender-based discrimination at work. Many women may decide to pursue more education to improve their prospects of advancement in order to combat these prejudices. However, this may cause additional difficulty as fewer women will be working overall.

Inclusion encompasses more than simply rainbow filters, women's day festivities, and numerical representation. The practise of inclusion must be mindfully woven into the fabric of an organisation that has grown vulnerable to the unintentional reinforcement of bias and discrimination. The threat to genuine fairness and inclusion still exists in the absence of inclusive management.

Diversity of gender in the workplace explores DIBE (Diversity, Inclusion, belonging, and Equality) trends and talks about ways to increase diversity at work. Enterprises and workplaces have no option but to adapt to agile, adaptable, and varied team structures as the standard as we prepare for the Fourth Industrial Revolution. Organisations can't just ignore women in the world's working-age population if they want to stay competitive.

According to statistics, even though we have made significant progress, there is still more work to be done before we can create a society where everyone is treated equally. In all of our efforts, we frequently concentrate on the fact that women do not have the same options and rights as men.

- Aren't men sometimes at a disadvantage and unable to make the same decisions as women?
- Are men truly permitted to choose unconventional careers?
- Do we tolerate guys who don't provide the majority of the family's income?

The gender wage disparity that most women experience in organisations across the world, not just in India, is another crucial factor. Even while there are more women in senior positions in their businesses, they tend to advance to these positions at a slower rate than white males do. Think about the best ways to create networks of professionals from various backgrounds in your industry.

Make the most of every chance to include more female role models and role models from a variety of backgrounds in marketing materials and online posts. One ad highlighted female engineers in honour of International Women in Engineering Day in 2019. Another suggestion may be to host and invite speakers to speak on diversity and inclusion in workplaces all around the world. To bring varied perspectives to the programme from all over the world, establish an internal global diversity and inclusion committee with global employee participation that has the support and endorsement of the leadership team. Make sure that everyone is represented on your diversity committees, including men, women, and individuals of various ages, races, and ethnicities.

Having more women in the workforce creates opportunities to employ underutilised or underutilised resources, which has a significant impact on productivity and the bottom line. DIBE advocates support the goal and can sponsor initiatives, serve as mentors, or speak up for financing and promotion as necessary. Let's face it, attempting to sell anything to a large gathering of people who may or may not be interested is never enjoyable. You don't have to do it alone, and it will really make you much more productive if you don't.

It's time to remove barriers surrounding the traditional male and female division of labour in the workplace and in our society since misconceptions about men have been developed by our culture and they restrict men's alternatives in life. The terrain and roadmap for creating an equitable world would be considerably different with this new strategy, and they could even be shorter than where we are now.

"In the workplace, men and women bring a variety of viewpoints to the table, fostering creativity and innovation that enables businesses to recognise and grasp new possibilities."

Teamwork can enhance team commitment and foster more group cooperation. According to research, women are better at interacting with others and communicating, which helps a diverse group of people perform at their best.

Females do not receive priority in receiving an education as compared to boys, which will damage their future and the chances they will have. Because employment are divided, there is a natural assumption that males are more suited than women to do particular tasks. Society as a whole is rife with unconscious bias, which has a big influence on gender disparity. The links to long-standing customs and traditions are another important factor contributing to the extreme gender inequality. According to government statistics, the number of incidents of sexual harassment reported at Indian workplaces grew by more than 50%.

It is essential to abolish pay concealment in order to advance gender equality. Organisations can advance significantly with enhanced wage transparency and compensation. To make it apparent how job position, seniority, and tenure effect each employee's salary, a formal pay structure should be created. The stigma associated with discussing pay can be broken down by this very knowledge.

How does gender inequity manifest itself?

According to UN Women, there is a 16% gender pay gap worldwide, which means that women's salaries are on average 84% of what men's salaries are. The disparity is considerably more pronounced among women of colour, immigrants, and mothers. A lack of community and support: even if women succeed in achieving the highest positions inside an organisation, they will still experience the cliché "It's lonely at the top."

There is a lot of room to increase gender diversity in the nation's manufacturing establishments. Women in the workforce provide organisations an advantage in the talent battle and foster the development of more collaborative, futuristic organisations. Organisations that choose to neglect diversity in the future do so at their own risk. Equal opportunity and female leadership bring about an effective, evidence-based transformation in organisations. In almost every profession worldwide, whether it be as a CEO or software engineer, the majority of women are still underutilised in terms of potential and leadership.

According to a McKinsey analysis, although making up over 50% of the global workforce, women only contribute 37% of the world's gross domestic product (GDP). This standard varies across the globe; for example, women account for only 17% of regional GDP production in India.

Therefore, there is a room for development in the area of women's employment. An organisation must promote equality at all levels in order to become gender diverse. Managers must concentrate on boosting gender diversity in business divisions and developing fun, cutting-edge work environments. Employees may transform their differences in thought, conduct, abilities, and expertise into new ideas and effective practises that advance a organisation when they have open, supportive interactions with coworkers and managers. The advantages of a diversified workforce might be numerous, using the underutilised and underexploited resource pool.

Opportunity is equal to time and a certain combination of circumstances, and the present is unquestionably the ideal time to be a woman. Women have historically been continuously marginalised in society, but things are changing. Women's empowerment organisations and ideas are already flourishing in the field. The situation becomes more convoluted if we focus on the whether or not women have equal opportunity.

This openness will enhance both organisational performance and morale. No of the gender, a workforce will only function more effectively if everyone thinks their time and efforts are being adequately valued. Removing obstacles to flexible working given that many women are prone to take on active parenting responsibilities, the lack of flexibility or stigma when it comes to variable working hours might constitute a barrier in the way of development for many female professionals. Women may believe they would be exempt from having children, while males are less likely to have similar anxieties in a situation that they can relate to. Women just need to know that when they return to work, they'll still have a job and a chance for advancement.

For a successful process, the ability to work remotely or with flexible hours should also be provided. Take a stand against aggressive and improper conduct. All employees, but particularly women, deserve to feel comfortable at work. Every organisation should be required to have strict procedures against sexual harassment and gender discrimination. In addition, businesses may develop a system that is easy to use for reporting harassment instances, and they can move quickly to discipline offenders. Such a culture can support an employee's sense of security and openness.

It offers a basic introduction of non-binary people, a business case for inclusion, a brief explanation of how non-binary people fit into existing equality legislation, and a prediction of potential future developments in the field. They do so from a global viewpoint that transcends specific difficulties encountered by Western civilizations.

With these varied viewpoints, the chapters examine interaction and structural mechanisms that might be employed to promote inclusion, going beyond demographic diversity. Working with and embracing non-binary people in the workplace benefits both the employer and the employee since it draws in and keeps younger non-binary workers while also upholding equality standards and helping to build an inclusive brand. It is based on an innovative study of non-binary inclusion in enterprises. This is an excellent opportunity for businesses looking to be inclusive of all genders in the workplace.

Take the founding of a tech start-up business by a group of college pals who all came from quite similar backgrounds. Every year, on a Sunday, the organisation staged a picnic where major events amongst the work teams took place which were followed by an employee appreciation awards presentation. This custom persisted as the business expanded quickly and hired a wide spectrum of skills. Some employees felt forced to choose between their faith and "being part of the team" because of their religious obligations and limitations on Sundays. The workplace picnic was intended to foster collaboration and convey appreciation, but several employees saw the opposite results. Some felt that the picnic's time and planned activities communicated the message "you and those who are like you do not truly belong here."

At their corporate picnic, the executives of the tech startup were alienating a portion of their employees, but they were unaware of it. For individuals whose origins and identities may be new to the majority at a workplace, it can be difficult to recognise what components of the work environment need to be adjusted to encourage inclusion. This is why proactively putting in place an inclusion programme is a crucial first step in developing an inclusive atmosphere.

We are motivated to fit in, and we are compelled to fit in in our own special way. And that strong need to fit in also has a lighter side, which is letting my true self show, leaning in, and being really engaged. Being a part of anything is an innate urge. Therefore, the key is to fulfil it at work and do it graciously. People speak about the future of employment, but it's already here. The momentum is beginning, and the result is obvious.

How can you stop it from happening? It will only become worse as technology and human resources at work enable us to be smart and distant at the same time. How can you speak out for them at a brainstorming session if they are not present in person but can still be included through a video? How can you share ideas at a table with others in a way that is inclusive? How do you ensure that the more subdued voices are heard, because 20% to 30% of the table will talk 80% of the time? What voice is therefore absent? Can you contemplate that at your employees meeting? Who should be there from what demography to ensure that our discussion produces the greatest results?

What can people managers do to create an inclusive team environment and, in turn, an inclusive organisational climate beyond simply being inclusive?

People managers, in my opinion, have an even greater duty to establish an atmosphere where everyone feels secure, respected, and welcomed, even though I believe that everyone inside the business has the capacity to promote an inclusive work environment. People Managers can act as role models for what behaviours are acceptable and what are not within their team, helping to shape the culture of that organisation. They are frequently the most powerful touch points. People It is crucial for managers to translate the idea of inclusion into actions and rituals that everyone can participate in.

It's crucial to work together among the organisation's diverse employee groups to fully utilise intersectionality. The discussion of how people managers may foster conversational safety in the next section responds to this query.

Bridging the knowledge gap with allies and conversational platforms. Recognizing the gap in behaviour and what drives it—which is frequently ignorance or inflexible mindsets—is one of the most important stages in creating an inclusive work environment.

The task of developing a culture and creating a safe space for candid, even uncomfortable conversations to break down psychological barriers to inclusion must be owned by team managers and leaders in order to ensure greater understanding, openness, acceptance, and subsequently accountability among team members to create a team climate that is safe for all.

Building inclusive environments requires developing areas for discourse, as demonstrated by learning from lived experiences: The first step that corporate leaders must take to establish more equitable workplaces is to listen to and learn about the lived experiences of their employees. One of the most effective tools managers can use is allies to reduce the complications that cloud challenging and painful dialogues about the lives of and bias against underrepresented groups. In truth, allyship is one tool to combat the continued emergence of bias and discrimination, while full fairness is still years away.

If organisations are serious about making workplace inclusion and belonging a lasting value and practise, inclusiveness as a quality is vital among people managers. People In addition to serving as role models, managers also act as bearers of ideals. The team dynamic and working environment are greatly impacted by how they engage with the team on a regular basis.

How are businesses preparing their people managers?

DIBE fosters a feeling of community that raises employee engagement and boosts organisational performance. This mindset is anchored by people managers, who also make sure their teams are led and supported. This entails examining our policies to make them more inclusive as well as committing to the community as a strong ally both inside and out. By regularly organising conscious and unconscious bias training for employees, particularly those at recruiting and managing levels, we have also made efforts to address incorrect behaviour. Additionally, systemic assistance like gender-neutral restrooms, and counselling services has been beneficial. Although we have come a long way, maintaining education is still important if we want to promote more diversity.

By implementing new inclusive recruiting standards, updating the job scopes to reflect inclusion, and creating a new onboarding programme that better meets the requirements of new recruits. To effect change, be aware of your zone of influence. Reward inclusive behaviour and chastise intolerant and discriminating actions and attitudes. A new inclusion program's structure and content must be tailored to your business's needs because every organisation is unique. Ensure that organisation executives are aware that inclusion means ensuring that each person's voice is heard, ideas are taken into account, and usefulness to the team is obvious.

- Managers should be trained in inclusion and held accountable for doing so.
- Create an inclusive council with real clout and authority.
- They value diversity and foster an environment where employees members feel free to be themselves at work.
- Determine the needs of underrepresented groups and provide them with the resources and assistance they require.
- Create a forum where employees may express their worries.
- Before implementing adjustments to enhance diversity.
- Benchmark important facets of your organisation's culture and understand the employee experience.
- The best way to determine whether your organisation has an inclusive culture is through everyday encounters, so keep that in mind.
- Encourage allies to be outspoken and visible.
- Create safe areas for communication to promote learning for you and your team.
- When unsure, seek advice from both leaders and colleagues.
- For organisations, diversity and inclusion are non-negotiable.
- Diverse teams may produce excellent outcomes, but only if they can work together in a welcoming environment where everyone is free to express themselves.

- Each team member must feel comfortable sharing their opinions openly or, to use the language of science, "feelings," in order to establish diverse teams that help any business achieve its goals.

How then do you capture and hold the leadership's interest?

Leaders have a responsibility to provide an atmosphere where individuals can be themselves, and they also have a responsibility to set an example for others by modelling respectful, receptive conduct that demonstrates the importance of every employee. Although creating an inclusive workplace culture has its merits, how crucial is inclusion to the success of an organisation? According to studies, organisations with inclusive cultures clearly outperform those without them, according to a study by Deloitte. It is a critical time for leaders to change the course of one of the most enduring issues in the workplace wage disparity.

People are often referred to as our greatest asset, but this can only be true if we foster an environment where they can flourish. The CEO or other organisational leader must set the tone for that in the organisation. Therefore, it is crucial that we have leaders in these organisations who are not threatened by that, who are not threatened by the growth of other people, but who are actually inspired by it and are prepared themselves to create that and to lead by example. This is because learning organisations or organisations that are open to growing people need leaders who are not threatened by that. A crucial part of leaving a legacy is mentoring. It's an essential strategy for helping future generations become more prepared and more productive in their daily lives. As a group and as a larger society, we do considerably better the more we invest in building communities of individuals who are successful and who are given the opportunity to improve.

"A sense of inclusion and belonging is fostered when an employer celebrates these holidays with the employees as a whole and everyone takes part in it."

For instance, top leadership team spent the time talking to every employee to gain their views on the schedule and the activities at the picnic after realising the stress that the picnic was giving certain workers. Each employee was particularly appreciated for their contributions, and great effort was made to put all of the practical suggestions they received into practise. This initiative was a crucial first step in developing a culture of inclusion, or a workplace where every person feels appreciated and included.

"Leadership should be focused on extending the ladder of opportunity for everyone." – Justin Trudeau

A relationship is more egalitarian if there is a little power imbalance and you have a very casual working connection with your coworkers, even if you are the manager. Understanding the dynamics of the power gap, especially as they relate to generational and cultural differences, can play a significant role in your effectiveness. For example, if there is a high power gap and you are the employee, you may perceive your leader as more of an authority figure and there is a huge gap between yourself and that corner office.

Your objective is to be a fluent leader as you navigate these disparities. An effective leader is able to collaborate with those who are different from them. Therefore, the following are the essential qualities that a fluent leader must possess.

- A person who is aware of both herself and other people, who is acutely aware of their own preferences while also beginning to recognise some of the distinctions among others. acceptance of complexity and ambiguity.
- Someone who consistently shows people they are loved and valued, especially in trying circumstances.
- Employee is someone who can bridge the power divide. Of course, someone who can innovate and show that they have what it takes to bring out the voices of others is also desirable.

I wish to strongly urge everyone to consider how they may master effective leadership techniques. Individuals sometimes assume that certain people are simply better at this than others when it comes to leadership and some of these training classes that we attend. Don't you think? And while, to some extent, this is true, I believe that we can all improve our ability to communicate effectively across generational and cultural boundaries as well as with people from diverse backgrounds. We can never be experts in everything.

We can never be experts in everything. It's really about how we engage diversity of thought, how do we work with people who think differently from us and who may even have different value judgments than us, how do we engage in that dialogue, and if we can get into a good consensual relationship. We continue to develop it as we meet someone who is different from us, as we work with another global office that we have never worked with before, and as we continually work with people who have different perspectives.

A solid commitment from the organisation's leaders as well as engagement at every level are necessary for the successful development of an inclusive culture. Even though there may be obstacles along the road, the efforts taken to establish an inclusive culture may boost employee engagement, retention, and contributions, all of which can materially enhance organisation results.

People managers are crucial in raising understanding of the LGBTQIA+ group, including its terminology, pronoun use, intersectionality, and the persecution it faces in society on a global scale. Recognize the presence of unconscious prejudices and attempt to eliminate them. Encourage the hiring of LGBTQIA+ individuals and make a contribution to inclusive policy.

> *"Employees won't be able to perform to their full capacity if they feel they can't be really themselves or express themselves as comes naturally to them."*

For fear of repercussions, employees who are different from the majority of their coworkers in terms of gender, sexual orientation, socioeconomic background, and generation sometimes conceal significant aspects of themselves at work. This is what those of us who work in the diversity and inclusion field refer to as "identity cover," and it makes it harder for people to express their emotions and desires, which leaves them open to quitting their organisations.

Other than women, the bulk of those most significantly impacted by the wage gap are LGBTQIA+ employees and people of colour. Organisations will need to take additional actions to reduce the growing wage gap, especially between those who perform the same job or role as well. Change must begin with the leaders if it is to be effective.

Along the way, remember to have fun and make sure that efforts are inclusive and pertinent to workers from all backgrounds.How can employers start a dialogue on stronger allyship in the workplace (and work towards it)?

Allyship gives LGBTQ+ workers the tools they need to achieve at their highest level each and every day, and it also gives us a chance to strengthen our sense of community for everyone.

How to promote diversity, inclusion, and a sense of belonging at work?

Uniqueness, integration, and belonging are gaining importance as industries try to develop workplaces that represent current demographic trends. In general, the world has become more diverse, but businesses haven't followed up, particularly when it comes to fostering an environment that is both culturally diverse and gender balanced. For business rebirth, tenacity, and inventiveness in the post-coronavirus world, organisations must change their focus from compliance to diversity and redefine the concepts of inclusion, diversity, and belonging from conformity to inclusiveness.

However, in the face of a pandemic, it has become necessary for all sizes of businesses to accept diversity, inclusion, and belonging management. This is especially true for local organisations that find it challenging to compete with large corporations, and it becomes even more challenging and expensive when organisations seek talent from all of these corporations. Now, even for brand-new hires, diversity is a top priority for the majority of organisations.

An employee will feel alone if they are going through personal struggles they don't feel comfortable sharing with others. They could find it difficult to focus on their work, feel as though no one is interested in them, and begin to consider leaving the organisation. However, productivity, retention rates, and morale all rise when employees members are treated with true respect and feel free to express themselves.

People Managers, who are the pillars of organisation culture, have the power to make considerable progress on the DIBE agenda. For instance, they may make sure that the LGBTQ+ group is actively hired into the workforce and assist in developing HR policies to create an inclusive workplace. Effective inclusion practises are implemented by great people leaders, such as making diversity more visible, giving diverse groups strategic assignments, letting them take turns running meetings, and actively seeking participation and suggestions from diverse groups to use their perspectives to make good decisions.

The culture of working from home is quite popular right now and has become the new standard for all of us. Uniqueness, integration, and belonging are gaining importance as industries try to develop workplaces that represent current demographic trends. Corporations are looking at every option to keep their operations consistent in the face of pandemics. Employees are favouring businesses that allow them to work permanently from home or until the epidemic is over. Prior to the pandemics, businesses had little interest in bolstering their IT infrastructure so they could provide employees the option of working from home, but now that it is necessary for businesses to prepare for the worst-case scenario, they must do so. To survive throughout this crisis, small businesses had no alternative but to carry on with the methods already in place. The recruiting procedure in small businesses underwent a major upheaval as soon as the epidemic struck.

Individuals of all gender identities, social backgrounds, traditional values, age, sexual preference, ethnicity, education, religion, and faith, as well as those with disabilities, can achieve their goals and pursue their passions thanks to the organisation's commitment to diversity, inclusion, and belonging.

The secret to inclusion is knowing who your employees are in reality. In a perfect world, all managers would be knowledgeable about their employees members and ensure that none were lost due to carelessness or ignorance. Employees who feel the need to hide some aspects of their identity may act in a fear-based manner at work. Examples given in the piece include a mother who is scared her coworkers would question her dedication to her career if she hangs up photographs of her kids; and a homosexual manager who is hesitant to bring his same-sex partner to a corporate function. By disguising a facet of their identity, these workers subtly believe that they do not entirely belong where they work because they hide a portion of who they are.

A solid diversity and inclusion plan may help organisations recruit top personnel and provide more innovative results. The profitability and value generation for the organisation increases with workplace diversity. Organisations are beginning to realise how important it is to prioritise and implement diversity and inclusion since it enhances the brand's reputation. For employees to have a feeling of connection to the organisation and to increase productivity, organisations need to foster a sense of belonging. It is insufficient to provide training materials and educate employees members on inclusivity. For inclusion to be successful, people must identify the essential components around which they might base new habits or microbehaviors. Real change will be feasible when these behaviours are put into practise in a setting that values open communication and constructive conflict. People's natural responses to being challenged in their views are fear and mistrust. While fear may be an effective motivator, it also encourages employees to have more limited viewpoints, the exact opposite of what is intended to foster a more inclusive workplace. Organisations must learn how to view problems through the prism of opportunity. Enhancing the influence of shared experiences has the potential to lead to positive change.

Organisations have traditionally excluded groups that are marginalised because of their ethnicity, age, gender identity, sexual orientation, language, or immigration status. The organisations that did recruit these groups also offered them no say in any meetings or decisions made at work. These marginalised workers can be encouraged to speak out and share their creativity and ideas through remote employment that provides collaboration tools and online skill training programmes. In virtual meetings, different viewpoints may be represented and incorporated, levelling the playing field for all employees.

Remote work alternatives provide organisations the flexibility to adopt a range of collaborative technologies and solutions that support a healthy and equitable workforce as they continue to make post-pandemic work decisions. Organisations that use a remote-first approach can secure the services of workers and contractors anywhere in the world while also promoting a diverse, equitable, and inclusive society.

In light of this, Statista, a business that does market research, and Forbes have collaborated to publish sixth annual list of the world's best employers. In order to assess which organisations excel in corporate influence and image, talent development, gender equality, and social responsibility, Statista polled 150,000 full-time and part-time employees from 57 countries who work for global corporations and institutions. Here is the list of the top 20 best employers worldwide as ranked in 2021.

<u>Name & It's Number Of Employees</u>

1. Samsung Group (266,673)
2. Microsoft (221,000)
3. IBM (250,000)
4. Alphabet (156,500)
5. Apple (154,000)
6. Delta Air Lines (80000)
7. Costco Wholesale (288000)
8. Adobe (25988)
9. Southwest Airlines (55093)
10. Dell Technologies (133000)
11. Lockheed Martin (114000)
12. Cisco Systems (79500)
13. BMW Group (118909)
14. Amazon (1608000)
15. Decathlon (100000)
16. Adidas (61401)
17. Airbus (125000)
18. Ferrari (4556)
19. Fraunhofer Society (30028)
20. Reliance Industries (230000)

In my opinion, anyone can start a movement. But I've also seen that for it to continue, there must be support from the leadership. Why? because so many suggestions for enhancing diversity, inclusion, and belonging call for organisational reforms at the structural level.

For instance, you'll need support for that direction if you want to alter how individuals are employed or recruited or if you want to guarantee accountability for diversity and inclusion. The following procedures will help you create buy-in.

- Firstly, conduct programs promoting diversity, inclusion, and belonging typically don't begin with top leadership. Many of the CEOs I speak with claim that the reason they supported diversity and inclusion was because their employees did. However, the word "employees" is plural; note the s. It's hard to argue that only one employee cares about this. Therefore, make sure to draw attention to the population you are affecting.
- Make sure your ERG is shown second. If no one is aware of your employee research group, having hundreds of people won't help. Social networking is a useful instrument for doing this. Consider how successful the #metoo or #bringbackourgirls campaigns were. Post pictures of your group participating in a rally or celebrating a victory. Additionally, you may invite speakers to discuss diversity with your ERG and post about it on social media. You're attempting to raise awareness of the problem, and decision-makers are interested in such things.
- Finally, send your requests up the chain of command. It's appropriate to start floating your objectives up the leadership ladder after you have an ERG and are well known inside the organisation. You may start by being open and honest with your direct manager, or you can ask your team whether any of their managers would be in favour of boosting diversity and inclusion. You can

speak to people in positions of authority if you know them.

However, I advise having open discussions before you put anything in writing. When you come across people who are on board, request their permission to write an email or memo outlining these crucial points. What you want, why it's good for business, and how they can assist. They can then send it up the chain in this manner. Decide what you would actually like from management, such as greater mentorship, more training, or equal compensation. You will be one step closer to making a successful shift after you determine what you're aiming towards.

A list of their programmes that promote inclusion, diversity, and belonging you're going to employ blind selection, so you must have a broad list of applicants with at least two women or people of colour in each pool. These two HR practises are among my favourites, but you cannot just email everyone about them. And to make matters worse, many businesses keep their employees in the dark.

"Teams with inclusive leaders who promote belonging frequently do excellent work because they feel encouraged and valued. When they believe they have a supporter within the organisation, these employees feel more comfortable speaking out and making choices. It's hardly surprising that workers under inclusive leaders are 2.5 times more likely to feel like they belong."

The employees at one organisation I worked with felt so in the dark that they frequently questioned me, "What are the diversity targets?" Although creating objectives is a good idea, this organisation hadn't done so. However, they were so secretive with their employees about what was happening that many assumed they were keeping something from them. It seems silly, but two years later, when I was employed by a totally different organisation, I was re-asked the identical question. There are few effective methods for disseminating information when it comes to communication.

- To control the message, first get allies. The majority of change management executives I've spoken with have advised me to select a few critical individuals within the organisation to speak with privately before sharing a message with everyone. Ask those you believe will support you for assistance in overcoming your worries or confusion. When you finally make your big announcement, your pals can assist in assuaging any worries that may arise once they eventually learn the workplace rumour. Hold a face-to-face discussion after that to go over the changes, why you're making them, how they will improve the organisation, what they are, and how they will affect various parties.
- Next, reinstil everything you already said about your DIBEs programme via email, memos, or social media. You may design a website, pamphlets, or even banners to promote diversity.
- If you're confident that everyone is aware of the changes, have another in-person meeting in a setting where anybody who wants to discuss them more is free to do so and express their worries, questions, or simply their responses. I would advise you to start by looking for those important allies if you were only going to make one move today. To identify potential allies for your communication plan, start bringing up the subject over lunch or in meetings. Your communication strategy will be far more successful if you can identify that one

person or those people.

Every business is capable of developing a culture of belonging. Regardless of how one's professional level affects each of these stages, I can't help thinking about how each one is doable. No step is too challenging or hard to carry out. Simply said, no organisation, large or small, should have an excuse for not fostering a sense of belonging among employees. Several research, methods, and concepts that aim to enhance inclusion and diversity in the workplace have arisen in recent years.

"We will only be successful in this change if individuals in positions of leadership shift away from command and control management approaches to reimagine how we view people, the most valuable resource in every enterprise."

- Dr. Amit Das

Driving Equality For A Better Performance Outcome In Your Organisation

"In today's interconnected and globalised world, it is now commonplace for people of dissimilar world views, faiths and races to live side by side. It is a matter of great urgency, therefore, that we find ways to cooperate with one another in a spirit of mutual acceptance and respect." – Dalai Lama

The way the world operates is changing quickly. Many people want to know what the best organisational approach is for their business. The emphasis of this chapter is on how to handle a hybrid workplace. The four main workforce strategies are as follows. The post-epidemic world's most frequently used tactic is hybrid work, which emerged from the worldwide pandemic.

A hybrid workplace is one in which employees have the freedom to decide how they will work the remaining business days of the week and are only required to visit a physical office four or fewer days a week. Running a hybrid work model might take many different forms, but the concept is always the same. Communication is crucial for businesses using a hybrid workplace, just like it is for companies using remote-first and 100% remote organisational methods. In order to improve cooperation and communication, many hybrid organisations use a virtual office platform because employees seldom, if ever, physically overlap 100% of the time.

The hybrid work schedule is one element that is especially exclusive to the hybrid organisational model. The physical on-site cadence that organisation personnel will adhere to is determined by this timetable. Frequently, a department, a boss, or a business policy will determine the particular cadence.

Many of us have been trapped in this forced work from home (WFH) social experiment for the past six or ten months, and during that time, there have been several discussions about the future of work, home working, and hybrid working. There have been numerous advantages to working from home, and many signs point to a hybrid future where most employees will spend a combination of days in the office and at home each week. But not every home is created equal. Many houses don't have reliable internet, enough room for a workstation, ergonomic seats, supportive surroundings, or just enough quiet. The overlap time for employees in the workplace may decrease in a hybrid future when employees work in the office two to three days per week. This means that organisations must strive harder to be more egalitarian in order to support all employees. I think there are a few significant prospects for workplaces in this regard.

I can recall being asked to repeat the organisation's most recent mission statement at a business conference years ago. They recognised the value of having a single vision and working together to achieve it. Every employee engagement model created both then and now has it at its core. If you ever wonder why employee engagement matters, all you need to do is glance at your financial sheet. This type of widespread employee engagement has a good effect on the future of your organisation.

How can one foster a sense of unity among a larger group of people, especially when employees work remotely?

You may do this by fostering a sense of belonging to a community where employees feel protected and appreciated, as well as by establishing shared information, ideas, and values. The kinds of employees you want working for your business are those that have easy access to channels of communication, are aware of what is expected of them by the organisation, and have clear personal objectives. These connected and involved employees are content in their positions and very productive, which in turn boosts organisation income and growth. The organisation's current market share and competitive position. Future organisational goals, including where they want to go and how they plan to get there. Employees must understand their place in this scenario.

The following are some of the best practises for cultivating a sense of belonging:

- Employees believe they can influence business decisions. Organisations must commit to listening if they want their employees to feel like they have some control over their job. The gender gap that exists in many organisations is a typical workplace example. In the workplace, favouritism and unjust project and promotion distribution are more frequently experienced by women.

- Promotions are a significant area where your organisation can fall short of its declared principles and your organisation's chance to exhibit its beliefs. Trust is damaged if your leaders emphasise the value of hiring women yet continue to pass them over for advancement. While showcasing the organisation as a supporter of genuine equality and diversity in the workplace, this also gives a chance to interact with a wider spectrum of potential hires who may have previously been dissuaded from joining.

Conquer any constrictive work environment and establish brand-new procedures and communication standards that let your employees participate in something bigger than themselves as your organisation comes to appreciate and value the distinctive experiences and viewpoints that each employee brings to the workplace.

"The most diversified and motivated workforces are found in the most successful organisations."

Studies suggest that companies with a high level of diversity perform 80% better. People are more engaged, more productive, and frequently more creative when they feel included and have the opportunity to realise their full potential. This development will be fueled by talent who feels completely accepted, appreciated, respected, and heard by their colleagues and their businesses. Building systems that value diversity in all of its manifestations, from identity and background to a variety of thinking, style, approach, and experience, and linking it to the bottom line, is also essential.

The analysis reveals that 87% of employees have a stronger sense of belonging when everyone is empowered at a organisation. These percentages fall to 72% and 68%, respectively, when only managers or senior leaders are able to identify their coemployees. What do you believe is necessary for them to feel secure enough, though? Well, the response is rather straightforward. When your employees feel important in the organisation, they will be more upbeat. Acceptance is the first step in building confidence, so it is your job as a manager to help your team members feel valued for their unique personalities, abilities, and viewpoints.

A business strategy known as "Remote-First" is built around the idea that working remotely is the preferred choice for most or all employees, but that regular team meetings still have importance. This usually includes yearly in-person gatherings and quarterly or monthly team retreats. Additionally, managers and employee are frequently granted access to satellite offices or co-working spaces to utilise as they see fit. The most recent organisational strategy is this one. It also emerged as a result of COVID-19, although not for reasons related to public health. Instead, when businesses and employees adopted full-time remote work, many wanted to keep it in place but still valued face-to-face engagement. The epidemic also affected the way many current employees lived and worked. Many individuals relocate to the suburbs or entirely new states.

Selecting a hybrid workplace strategy has a lot of advantages. These advantages apply to both the employee and the employer. Employee satisfaction, for example, has secondary advantages that improve the organisation's culture, morale, and productivity. Hybrid work, at its most basic level, aims to provide more freedom while preserving some of the advantages of an in-person workplace.

Employers wished to maintain a physical bond between employees while also ensuring workplace safety. According to a 2022 research report by management consulting organisation McKinsey, the model has evolved from being a short-term public health plan to the default norm for the majority of US employees. To meet the demands of today's workforce, remote and hybrid work have rapidly increased in popularity. Employees are very opposed to going back to full-time on-site employment five days a week after two years of working from home at least occasionally. A return to 100% in the workplace is no longer realistic for many businesses. In a nutshell, hybrid working takes place in organisations that use a hybrid workplace strategy. These two phrases are interchangeable and frequently used to contrast the organisation and the person. The employee has complete discretion to determine their own on-site work schedule under this form of timetable.

Whether they are at the office or working remotely, employees may effortlessly engage in a hybrid workspace. These hybrid workplaces, also known as virtual workspaces, are frequently developed by businesses in order to facilitate cooperation and improve communication. Here's an illustration of a mixed workstation.

Organisations typically provide employees with some sort of direction on how many in-person days they should work during a specific time frame. This figure is determined on a weekly, monthly, quarterly, or annual basis depending on the organisation. Despite being less common among hybrid businesses, this hybrid work schedule has several distinctive advantages. Many organisational psychologists and workplace specialists advise against having a tight timetable. This is so because the advantages for the employee frequently result in advantages for the organisation that are higher. Employees appreciate this arrangement because it gives them more flexibility in their lives and, more significantly, it gives them more control over how they do their in-person work. This helps them to perform to their highest potential and make the most of their in-office time.

Employees can pick their working environment and hours under this policy based on their goals. This also entails that personnel in bigger hybrid organisations may switch between physical workplaces at any time of the year. This creates a relationship of trust between management and the employee and eliminates the need for in-person meetings. As it allows employees to adjust to their unique family demands, such as moms with small children, or physical needs, such as disability accessibility, this approach is most suited for creating an inclusive workforce. More applicants can comply with the corporate workplace plan when there is more freedom.

There is a greater chance for physical collaboration and team-building exercises. It provides employees with a weekly routine that is predictable, allowing them to organise appointments and errands. Planning and predicting the amount of office space needed is simple for management. The distinction between remote work and hybrid work is clear. To put it simply, remote work is a part of hybrid work. Employees will spend a portion of their workdays working remotely in a hybrid workplace. A predilection for remote work has been embraced by several organisations, including remote-first and entirely remote organisational designs. In these tactics, employees mostly or exclusively do business from their homes or other preferred locations.

This is a strategy where the business focuses on allowing employees to work remotely while also bringing the team together for bigger events and maybe granting access to shared physical workplaces. Businesses have begun referring to this work policy as "remote first" because of the rising popularity of this organisational approach and the fact that "remote-first hybrid work model" is a mouthful. Airbnb is a famous business that has used this tactic. Here is a comprehensive guide for a remote-first workplace approach if you want to learn more about the concept. According to research from workplace planning consultant Global Workplace Analytics, using a hybrid working paradigm where employees are out of the office 50% of the time will save the typical employer over $11,000 a year. This cost decrease is mostly attributable to lower expenditures for office space, office equipment, and utilities.

Although Google's public policy still favours an office-first hybrid approach, 10,000 Google employees have actually been given the choice of permanent remote employment. More than 85% of requests for remote employment are accepted, according to the business. It gives employees the freedom to select the days they work remotely. Reduced commuting times and emissions from workplace heating and cooling are two benefits of hybrid employment.

According to their data, employees between the ages of 18 and 34 are over 60% more likely to leave their jobs than those between the ages of 55 and 65 are nonbinary and female employees. In comparison to men, women are 10% more likely to resign if they are not given the option of working in a hybrid environment. For employees who self-identify as nonbinary, the percentage almost doubles to 18%.

How a hybrid workplace may strengthen a organisation's diversity, inclusion, belonging, and euality strategy (DIBE)?

Leading management consulting organisation McKinsey has spent a lot of time investigating the effects of hybrid work (DIBE). Although not unexpected, their findings are intriguing. A organisation's DIBE strategy will benefit by providing non-fixed five-day in-office work schedules. The use of hybrid work models is growing. Hybrid work has quickly emerged as the leading organisational strategy in the United States between the years 2020 and 2022. The working population is experiencing large-scale regional, generational, and cultural changes as a result of this rapid surge.

Flexibility is something that employees value and want more of. According to a 2022 poll by Envoy, a provider of workplace visitor management software, 63% of employees believe that flexibility would give them a sense of increased control. A mixed work schedule provides employees with a lot of freedom. Employees can achieve a better work-life balance thanks to the possibility of working from home. Frequently, this entails spending more time with loved ones. Freedom of choice is what leads to higher satisfaction in the workplace, regardless of how a employee spends their time. Higher levels of employee loyalty and retention also help the organisation, which is another advantage of these factors.

A worry about fairness is one of the difficulties that remote-optional businesses, also known as remote-friendly businesses, encounter. These businesses employ hierarchical organisational structures that prioritise on-site presence yet are open to hiring remote employees. It might be challenging for employees to know when and how to encourage face-to-face communication. Employees have limited personal options. Employee animosity as well as productivity losses may result from this. Lack of visibility can cause management problems. greater difficulties in adhering to the rules of the U.S. Equal Employment Opportunity Commission with respect to employees who require accommodations. Fairness-related issues When a organisation uses a fixed hybrid work paradigm, junior employees frequently voice concerns about unfairness across management levels over how tightly the set hybrid work schedule is implemented.

There is very little flexibility for employees to work from home. Some managers have expressed concern about a "zoom ceiling," a term borrowed from "glass ceiling" that refers to a lack of career advancement for employees who need special remote accommodations. According to studies, most employees are dissatisfied with this approach and, in certain instances, would leave their organisation if it favoured in-office work. The dual work approach includes working from home once more. Employees can work from anywhere they choose during their off-work hours, including from home or a coffee shop. Working from home and remote work are now interchangeable terms that apply to both employees and employers.

The average American employee commutes for $8,466 annually. As a result, the typical employee who works a schedule of two office days and three work from home days will save more than $5,000 annually. However, employees should expect additional cost savings beyond communication because buying food and beverages in bulk at grocery shops is far less expensive than doing so at delis, lunch places, and other similar establishments.

Although working a few flexible days each week or month remotely is permitted, employees are required to be present in the office on a daily, weekly, or monthly basis. This hybrid work environment most closely resembles a comprehensive on-site organisational plan. Most notably, Google attempted to use this tactic but was met with fierce employee pushback and immediately reversed course. In the event that demographic or socioeconomic shifts have a greater impact on the workforce, businesses that are adopting hybrid working will be well-positioned. Organisations utilising a hybrid workplace will be able to change to delivering more in-office or remote work dependent on future demands because of the gap between in-office and totally remote employment. For many organisations, adopting a mixed work paradigm permanently required essentially no implementation.

There are many problems that managers and executives must overcome, but some are unique to managing a hybrid business. Here are some specific difficulties with hybrid functioning and suggestions for overcoming them.

- Even while it can appear straightforward, every business must carefully assess which model is ideal for their particular business. Management may alienate employees if they choose the incorrect model. It is advisable to solicit opinions from a variety of team members within the business. Employee opinions of the ideal hybrid work paradigm are significantly influenced by demographic factors.
- Hybrid businesses must make sure they are not unintentionally fostering silos and knowledge loss by

not assembling all employee everyday in one place. The most effective hybrid workplaces foster seamless communication between local and remote team members. The ideal approach to take in this situation is to use virtual office software.

- Managers and HR teams will aim to maintain employeess' sense of community with one another at all times. One of the few issues raised by hybrid employees, isolation and disengagement, should be treated extremely seriously. The key to keeping employees feeling informed and fostering team ties is to create virtual water cooler moments.

- Many managers are concerned that having less face-to-face time will make it harder for them to supervise their employees. Here, trust and recruiting excellent personnel is the greatest tactic. Giving employees authority is favourably received by them. Excellent leaders give their employee the confidence they need to do the job.

The incorporation of this inclusion component has changed diversity initiatives during the past ten years. Companies understand that if everyone doesn't feel like they can participate completely or be themselves, they can't profit from diversity. This makes sense, yes? People won't share their diverse perspectives with you if they don't feel like they have anything to contribute or if they feel like they just need to fit in. In fact, data shows that they're much more likely to leave your organisation because it feels terrible to not belong and is exhausting to be someone else. Diversity must succeed via inclusion. Recall that diversity is getting the right individuals in the door, and inclusion is accepting them and allowing them to be themselves as we continue to discuss diversity and inclusion.

It may be argued that the world has changed since the blatant manifestation of brutality and inhumane treatment of individuals who are not like us, as seen in several periods of human existence. Even while these more violent forms of prejudice are no longer overt in our culture, they nonetheless persist, albeit in a more covert manner and with the same negative effects. The majority of organisations would want to think of themselves as being devoid of bias or as having reached a point where they are. But more often than not, this might be an idealistic picture that could be a challenge when trying to unlearn some harmful habits. For this reason, it wouldn't be more advantageous to actively identify and call out these biases as they occur, since only then would our DIBE outcomes noticeably alter. Here are a few strategies for conducting a successful DIBE leadership programme in your organisation.

- When formulating a DIBE strategy, an organisation must focus on the expectations of its workforce.
- A organisation must listen to its customers. Giving your people a voice again and making room for the experiences of varied groups at work are two important factors in this.
- Meeting other people's perceptions of what is right is important for doing what is right, after all. These are components of a framework where organisations are motivated to bring about genuine, lasting change in addition to being mindful about their DIBE. After all, pursuing diversity targets and relying on thorough statistics are merely the first steps toward what more

organisations can do to create an environment that values diversity and fortifies an inclusive culture.

Due to obstacles like unconscious prejudice, advancing diversity is more difficult than finishing a standard change. Due to this, it is even more crucial for businesses to have a strong transformation programme that specifically targets unconscious bias and that the leadership team is committed to the effort. This may call for opposition from within or outside the organisation. Even when best practises are consistently followed and best intentions are presumed and put into effect, data-driven diversity programmes can frequently uncover unconscious biases that hinder the exercise of sound judgement throughout the organisation.

On the HR side, there are hiring procedures, selection criteria, and methods for deciding who gets promotions, who has access to training opportunities, and what kinds of perks are offered. The preventative strategy in each of these is to steer clear of prejudice. Of course, people shouldn't be treated unjustly. And you don't want some HR procedures to adversely affect particular groups disproportionately. You may argue that it is fair since everyone is treated equally if there is a dearth of daycare. However, because women are still more often the primary carers, it affects them more than it does males, particularly black women and women of colour. Then there is the matter of promotions.

How can you encourage behaviours that enable women or people of colour to compete on an even playing field?

These could include hiring procedures that encourage diversity or development initiatives that specifically target underrepresented groups. Simply encouraging more openness can result in a more diverse and equal workplace.

You should steer clear of cultural behaviours like bullying, harassment, and microaggressions that exclude or devalue particular groups of individuals. On the other hand, you want to advocate for inclusive programmes so that everyone feels like they belong and is confident in their ability to be themselves. Keep these questions in mind as you start to think about how your needs and aspirations fit within this matrix.

First, where in your organisation do the biggest demographic inequalities exist? Does it affect top executives more than entry-level employees? Next, ask yourself: What diversity imperatives do you have? To encourage more women, perhaps a rise in the proportion of individuals of colour? Naturally, your programme could meet each of these objectives, but it's important to remember what diversity means to you personally. Third, and perhaps most crucially, what tools do you have at your disposal to really carry out your objectives? Some modifications, like development, might be quite pricey. Others, like enhancing transparency, can be done rather cheaply. You should also think about your degree of assistance. You probably won't change the makeup of the board of directors if HR agrees with you but upper management disagrees. Why don't you try to come up with one opportunity in each of the topics I discussed to start? You wish to raise and reduce one structural issue and one cultural issue. And it will prompt you to consider what your DIBEs program's core needs are.

Although there are hierarchies in place, all employees work in a common area with amenities that were constructed specifically for their needs. Think of an app that encourages you to have lunch with five brand-new coemployees that you have never met before. In order to meet socially, an office app is curating various profiles across hierarchy, ethnicity, colour, gender, and sexual orientation. These relationships might be used to create reading clubs, affinity groups, and other safe places that the future workplace sponsors to really encourage interaction and understanding among its employees. And soon, all employees will feel comfortable bringing their true selves to work since they are familiar with coemployees who are not part of their social or racial group.

When will we no longer consider gender equality to be a problem?

There are things we can do to create a truly inclusive workplace where women's advancement doesn't have unintended repercussions. To promote gender equality and give women equal opportunity at home and at work, enough has been said, done, and is being done. It is unnecessary to reiterate the urgent necessity to transform our cultural and societal norms in order to promote gender parity in all spheres of life.

It is common knowledge that women perform three times as much unpaid care work as men do globally. Additionally, they deal with prejudices and inequities at work that limit their opportunities for advancement. However, despite countless attempts and well-intentioned interventions, the issue still exists.

As demonstrated by research and real-world examples, the success of an organisation depends on its capacity to draw in and empower people with varied viewpoints. Businesses that encourage a variety of genders on their executive teams are more likely to be profitable and competitive. Numerous studies have demonstrated the numerous benefits that diverse representation across all levels of a business can provide, including enhanced profitability and innovation, stronger governance, and improved problem-solving skills.

The creation of new workplace designs that allow easy physical movement for people with disabilities is one shift that practitioners of investing will need to take into consideration. Integrating doing good with organisation operations and advancing corporate goals is referred to as integration. We frequently have a workforce shortage since we work in the hotel sector, and as travel and foreign business activities pick up, this problem will become much more acute. It was a good moment to question our own views while embracing inclusive hiring since it allowed us to reach out to more applicants and other organisation divisions, expanding our reach and creating a win-win situation.

Think about supporting organisations like equal rights advocates, a non-profit devoted to improving women's rights in the workplace, through donations or by collaborating with them. The group is renowned for advocating for laws to outlaw discrimination against women. Review and reduce the gender wage gap in your own organisation to be a change agent. You can take the following steps to create a truly inclusive workplace where women's advancement does not have unintended consequences:

- Ensure that men and women have equal access to and participation in all educational programmes.
- Assisting high-potential female leaders in their pursuit of positions of leadership.
- Establish male mentorship programmes and appoint female executives to serve as mentors.

- Review your coaching and mentoring initiatives and see whether only men are serving as other men's mentors. Men with working spouses or partners should be nominated to lead and drive DIBE initiatives.
- Inquire whether the men being questioned have working partners and, if not, why not. This will reveal any innate prejudices they may have.
- Make sure there is pay equity when job offers and promotions are made.
- Ensure flexibility and a healthy work-life balance.
- Disprove and report prejudices.

Every day, everyone of us has the chance to build a more inclusive and equitable society. Make the most of those in order to collectively close the gender gap. The struggle for equal compensation for equal effort is still going on! Champions may significantly affect how a programme is viewed, especially in your leadership. One successful tactic is to request their assistance in promoting a course or event by becoming a sponsor. Don't undervalue the importance of connections in the success of your programme. Request that your sponsors personally invite audience members, particularly other influential people. Most individuals understand that it's advantageous to be connected to initiatives that a business values. By demonstrating how the occasion, programme, or approach fits with their personal and business brands, you may inspire your sponsor. Include their involvement in the creation of the project or programme to give them a stake in the outcome. For instance, ask the influencer for a referral if you're employing an external consultant. Alternately, sit down with them and ask what they believe is most crucial for DIBE in your environment.

Equal pay for equal labour would provide employees, especially women, the chance to support their well-being and take care of their loved ones without having to make sacrifices. Future hybrid workplaces must offer equal assistance to every individual in a varied workforce. The need to reconsider the condition of diversity, inclusion, belonging, and equality in your places has never been greater.

You may gain a deeper understanding of your organisation by helping this individual come up with a list of DIBE assets based on their sphere of influence. The terminology employed by your team or organisation that is consistent with accepted DIBE concepts is another thing to consider. Your organisation probably already has a specific webpage or statement outlining your dedication to diversity and inclusion. Building on these already-existing principles will help to reinforce the idea that DIBE is everyone's responsibility rather than something that needs to be invented from scratch.

Knowing that women are disproportionately underrepresented in the workforce and make much less money than men does not tell the whole story. The bigger issue for executives is to examine closely at their own organisations and assess if these disparities are dividing distinct labour groups. Engage an independent auditor with expertise in examining and resolving income discrepancies in your organisation, and collaborate with them to develop solutions.

In order to comply with universal access regulations, sometimes known as disability codes, newer office buildings must include assisted areas, ramps, unisex wheelchairs, ambulant restrooms, tactile signs and warnings, and more. Older structures or workplaces frequently do not adhere to these modern regulations, which restrict job chances for people who would be adversely affected by their absence. By investing in these facilities, management sends a clear message that every employee must have equitable access to the resources that support their job by investing in these facilities to accommodate all people with disabilities or regardless of their sexual orientation.

Perhaps you're doing a wonderful job of diversifying the leads you generate for your employment programme. Don't be hesitant to emphasise that. I can't emphasise enough how crucial it is to create an internal and external business identity that has diversity and inclusion at the centre. Of course, the voice of the leadership is essential if you want to truly match your organisation's narrative with DIBE ideals. Even if you have a compelling textual message, it still needs a face. Encourage your supporters and other key figures to speak out in favour of these principles. Starting with champions, you then move on to corporate principles before bringing the champions back in. You get the concept, I believe. Without individuals to live them and give them a voice, values are meaningless.

Each employee has the option to pick their working environment for the day based on the tasks at hand, rather than supervisors having offices and the others having desks. It could be a workstation, a calm area for concentrated work, an office for private conversations, or a meeting spot. Colleagues can have casual conversations in the coffee bar, and everyone has access to the central service locations for printing and office supplies. The not-so-new idea of activity-based working offers a lot more freedom and prevents communication barriers, but it also offers the opportunity to share all workspaces among all employees, encouraging a feeling of parity in the workplace.

"No culture can live, if it attempts to be exclusive." – Mahatma Gandhi"

A number of policies that further promote inclusive corporate we want to foster an atmosphere free from harassment, bullying, and discrimination while also promoting and upholding a safe and healthy workplace. We have always encouraged our employees to strike a good balance between their family and professional lives. As a result, we provide flexible scheduling to meet employee demands.

The majority of men do not participate in DIBE projects at work, and at one extreme, they may even feel openly intimidated and hostile by the shifting cultural landscape. Others, however, could lack the will to adapt since they are just aware of the general advantages of variety. Change is no longer necessary. Belonging is the call to action we need right now. It is the means by which we can make the men in positions of authority our partners in the fight against institutional racism, sexism, and all forms of workplace discrimination. We can work together to create a better workplace where everyone feels like they belong by using the ideas from this chapter. This provides you with a thorough understanding of the focus groups that are now popular as well as individual research on unconscious bias, global diversity, equality, and equity. It guides you in overcoming difference and prejudice while enhancing equality.

How do you think businesses can help women stay in the workforce?

The epidemic has placed us in an uncharted situation with no precedent or strategy. All employees have found it tough at this time, but female employees have found it more difficult since they continually struggle to achieve a work-life balance. I've come to feel that flexibility is the key to finding a balance between career, family, and one's particular existence as a woman. The concept of working from home has evolved for working women who are also moms or wives. Organisations must, therefore, make sure that women are empowered, trusted, and understood. In exchange, it greatly contributes to fostering a sense of loyalty and belonging to the organisation. Managers must be willing to adapt to traditional methods of working and adopt new ones, as well as to have meaningful dialogues with their employees and be transparent about their issues. It is crucial for managers to cultivate an environment where employees can be themselves and do their best job.

According to a multi-year study conducted by McKinsey & Co., women in entry-level professions have fewer opportunities to advance to first-level management positions. As a result, the expression "broken rung" was coined. How can organisations promote greater diversity and inclusion among the workforce and eliminate the "broken rung" that has been further harmed by the pandemic?

Although the broken rung is a major problem, I think it requires a different approach. In the majority of organisations, executives place a strong emphasis on promoting women into leadership roles, which often focuses attention on the pipeline rather than advancement. The initial promotions, though, are where the actual issue resides. To guarantee the healthy progression of the pipeline, it is crucial that we invest in women at lower levels. It is good to see fewer women leave the workforce if they are mentored, acknowledged, and given the correct chances early in their careers. In parallel, women should take bold measures to guarantee that there are no broken rungs in the ladder of opportunity for men and women.

Female employees must consider how women may offer value, participate in meetings with fresh perspectives, get their hands dirty, and assist with projects of all sizes, even if they fall outside of their purview. The most effective leaders today are those who can inspire, and I organisationly think that we all have the capacity to do so.

According to a Pew Research Center study, women earn 84% less than men, as has been repeatedly emphasised. Due to the epidemic, women now face more home responsibility demands, and those who return to work are subject to pay reductions for their extended absence from the workforce. How could businesses modify their pay policies to promote increased employees participation? A: Organisations must foster a culture that supports the hiring of women. In particular, for those juggling various jobs and obligations at work and at home, policies like Flex Work that let women work part-time are crucial. Organisations are attempting to use gender-neutral greetings such as "hey friends," "hello colleagues," and "workforce as opposed to manpower."

"I support this action. The DNA of inclusion and diversity should be woven into all organisational policies. It is crucial to teach our managers about unconscious bias and how harmful it is to an organisation's success since gender stereotyping is a significant problem that I have worked with."

You need to understand why the stakes are so high for our society and the bottom line. It will instruct you on how to bring about change, make change, and turn change into money. This chapter offers a fresh, capabilities-based approach to workplace equality. In addition to helping people feel like they are being treated fairly, this method highlights steps that organisations may take to assess and enhance the ways in which they support equality for all of their members. This groundbreaking chapter gives fresh perspectives on how equality in the workplace may be pursued and accomplished, moving beyond equal opportunities and diversity management techniques. I will share real life examples of like Honda, BP, Google, Apple, and Coca-Cola to illustrate real-world methods while also addressing theoretical discussions and practical applications. Legal, sociological, and neoliberal economic advancements, as well as neoliberal economic thinking and concerns, have all contributed to diversity, inclusion, belonging and equality becoming aspects of companies. The #MeToo movement, and gender pay discrepancies all appear to have finally convinced every organisation that real change is required. Numerous studies have shown that senior management teams that are really varied and eclectic are the most successful and effective.

How are you fostering an inclusive working culture?
How do you include DEI throughout your whole employee lifecycle?

We have considerably improved our work environment for employees via the use of better productivity tools, especially in the areas of hiring, employee training, communication, and wellbeing. Technology enables us to establish an open, truthful, and anonymous feedback method. Managers may then make informed judgments about the business and human resources. Additionally, adopting best in class tools with the active participation of top management and key leaders may have an impact. Examples include design thinking and open space technology. According to millennials, workplace diversity is the blending of various origins, experiences, and viewpoints. They also think that utilising these disparities to one's advantage is what spurs creativity.

"Train individuals sufficiently so they can depart. If you treat them nicely, they won't want to leave. " This Richard Branson quotation is more applicable in the present day than it was ten years ago.

We in the HR leadership know how important people are to any business. The wellbeing of a organisation's teams closely relates to that organisation's performance. No matter their gender or socioeconomic status, a significant portion of this employee's welfare indicates that they must be treated appropriately and with the highest respect at work. Because of this, a coordinated strategy for diversity, inclusion, belonging, and equality (DIBE) is essential for every business that aspires to be a great place to work. More than 80% of millennials feel that an employer's policies on diversity, equality, and inclusion have a significant impact when determining whether to work for them, according to a new PwC poll on removing obstacles to diversity. This change has taken place as a result of the favourable effects DIBE has demonstrated having on performance, innovation, and brand. According to millennials, workplace diversity is the blending of various origins, experiences, and viewpoints. They also think that utilising these disparities to one's advantage is what spurs creativity.

Employees who experience a sense of "oneness" are inspired to work harder each day, which improves both the organisation's ability to solve problems and its financial performance. According to the impact of diversity on groups, more diversity is linked to improved collaboration and idea generation. By having new talent and innovative ideas, it gives businesses the chance to spot the newest trends. It serves as a major motivation for employees members, lowers absenteeism, and fosters a sense of community in both real and virtual offices.

Employee involvement is crucial for developing an empowering organisation culture. Employees who interact with individuals from various cultures learn about other cultures and feel appreciated. In order to advance DIBE, business conglomerates are establishing diversity councils, hosting webinars, panel discussions, learning and development (L&D) modules, seminars, catch-up sessions, and management training programmes. Looking inside, it's crucial to remember that during both pandemic waves, logistics specialists risked their lives while working against the clock to bring happiness, health, and safety to our doorstep. In such a situation, it is essential to provide employees' wellbeing and mental health with greater attention than ever before.

An ideal gender balance in the workforce ensures that decision-making, innovation, creativity, and knowledge-sharing processes run smoothly inside a business. To secure their growth in the current environment, businesses must carefully reorganise their employment policies. For many years, the ratio of frontline employees has been skewed towards one gender. However, it is reassuring to know that there are now significantly more women working in the logistics sector. In 2020 research from Gartner, women now make up 39% of full-time employees in supply chain roles, up from 35% in 2016. Organisations are dedicated to altering women's futures at work over time by offering them options for upskilling and educational training. Additionally, they are assisting them in breaking the stereotype of "men-dominated" professions and preparing them for leadership roles. Additionally, in order to make sure that both existing and potential employees are aware of the racial makeup of their organisation, executives perform yearly monitoring and diversity audits.

High-performing organisations place a high priority on the crucial business principles of diversity and inclusion. They put a lot of effort into creating conditions that promote employee success. Companies are propelled toward a better and more promising future through diversity. We in the HR leadership know how important people are to any business. The wellbeing of a organisation's teams closely relates to that organisation's performance. No matter their gender or socioeconomic status, a significant portion of this employee's welfare indicates that they must be treated appropriately and with the highest respect at work. Because of this, a coordinated strategy for diversity, inclusion, belonging, and equality (DIBE) is essential for every business that aspires to be a great place to work. More than 80% of millennials feel that an employer's policies on diversity, equality, and inclusion have a significant impact when determining whether to work for them, according to a new PwC poll on removing obstacles to diversity.

We think organisations that employ sustainable DIBE strategies may provide significant outcomes. Organisations that have implemented a diversity-first HR approach have consistently demonstrated superior performance, notably in the areas of revenue creation, employees retention, and employee engagement. Each individual on your team is unique and needs to be treated as such. A wise leader will understand this and take appropriate action. We've established the significance and consequences of cultural development. However, in order to maintain this culture, the leader must speak with employees members often and comprehend their requirements for the development of the team and business. For employees to feel more confident, the team leaders must recognise and encourage their uniqueness. For instance, by avoiding collective thinking, which can sometimes exclude other ideas, leaders can promote individuality. The team's leaders can solicit each member's viewpoint and urge them to participate in the team's expansion. They can further assess the employee's aims for assistance by recognising the employee's conduct. It is the most effective technique to boost team productivity and establish a good environment.

This change has taken place as a result of the favourable effects DIBE has demonstrated having on performance, innovation, and brand. According to millennials, workplace diversity is the blending of various origins, experiences, and viewpoints. They also think that utilising these disparities to one's advantage is what spurs creativity. Employees who experience a sense of "oneness" are inspired to work harder each day, which improves both the organisation's ability to solve problems and its financial performance.

How can organisations create a level playing field for all employees?

People assemble when they feel a sense of belonging. A truly diverse organisation that prioritises inclusion while honouring and valuing diversity. We opted to concentrate our thoughts on women in the workforce today because they easily make up almost half of the workforce in most organisations worldwide, and because we are celebrating women this whole month. The recruiting and HR business, like other industries, is undergoing fast change right now as new laws are passed, workplace empathy best practises are developed, and innovative approaches to boosting productivity in the middle of a pandemic are discovered. Diversity is more important than ever in modern society. In order to prevent stagnation and rigidity and to demonstrate that we are genuinely eager to modify the behaviours, policies, and programmes in our workplaces, it is crucial that we comprehend the notions of diversity and inclusion as crucial measures to welcome and build a sense of belonging.

According to ManpowerGroup, talent shortages are at their worst point in the previous ten years. 40% of US businesses say it's hard to find suitable candidates to fill open positions. This percentage is around 80% in Japan, but it is more like 20% in China. If a shortage of talent is the main motivation behind your diversity programmes, that justification might not hold water in other nations. The fourth reason is to reflect on your consumer base in order to better connect with them. Once more, remember to think about who you are serving in each location.

The key is that diverse viewpoints enable individuals to counteract groupthink and provide original, cutting-edge, and often even more precise answers. In order to effectively adapt your organisation's commitment to diversity to a global setting, it is crucial that you can clearly state why you care about it. By doing so, you can adapt your diversity strategy to each cultural setting while still upholding the fundamental principles of diversity in your business.

According to Glint's study, perceptions of leaders' inclusiveness are substantially connected with followers' trust in them, which is frequently a major motivator of involvement. In the end, a leadership commitment to inclusiveness encourages better outcomes for both the organisation and its people. Inclusion is a dynamic, systemic process. It is not a training course or a one-time occurrence. Every encounter that takes place in the process of doing work has the potential to create (or destroy) it. In the whole organisation, upskilling is essential. I recommend that enterprises need to stop operating in isolation and start collaborating in order to maximise the impact of DIBE projects. In the past, efforts for gender, LGBTQI, and other categories might have been made, but in today's age of globalisation, diversity encompasses more than just these categories. The concept of intersectionality examines how factors such as race, sexual orientation, socioeconomic class, age, disability, and gender might combine to disadvantage individuals. The rising complexity of businesses like DIBE needs organisations to expand their capacity for cooperation by making wise near-term judgments about how HR teams can successfully execute complex events.

In order to assist women in achieving their full potential on the personal, professional, and career fronts, it is crucial to research the different possibilities and problems affecting women's empowerment. Promoting women's inclusion, diversity, and equity following the COVID-19 Pandemic offers pertinent theoretical frameworks and the most recent empirical research results in the areas of diversity, equality, and inclusion, promoting women's empowerment. It studies women's contributions to sustainability and future development and improves and enlightens how women are perceived both individually and collectively.

In addition, PwC concluded its Women in Work Index research, which provides a chance to consider the very real effects of the COVID-19 epidemic on women's lives, careers, economic well-being, and general wellness, as well as on the future. In reality, the epidemic has caused the world's two years of advancement to be undone in correcting gender pay gaps. In the previous five years, businesses have lost $223 billion due to employee turnover caused by cultural issues. For a more just and fair society, it is imperative that we consistently show up and create equity for everyone in our recruiting procedures, business communications, and other areas.

Working from home has produced enormous benefits in terms of employee productivity, contentment, and office atmosphere two years later. Organisations were obliged to restructure team interactions to promote diversity, equity, and inclusiveness as a result of the pandemic's widespread disruption (DIBE) efforts. Many businesses made use of remote and hybrid work arrangements during this economic downturn to foster a diverse, egalitarian, and inclusive workplace. The advantages that followed include improved internal efficiency and access to larger talent pools. Organisations may foster a more inclusive working environment that caters to the needs of many marginalised groups by adopting a remote-first mentality.

What actions can businesses take to guarantee that women are devoted to their jobs?

Every organisation should endeavour to provide a safe environment at work, but this is only achievable when there is zero tolerance for harassment of any kind and non-compliance. A crucial element in creating a safe workplace is having an open-door policy with confidentiality and no retribution. All employees must be granted flexibility, and they must be allowed the freedom to do their tasks without interference or bias. For all employees' emotional and mental wellness, trained counsellors in employee assistance programmes who can help them regardless of their gender roles are essential. Employee resource groups are crucial in developing a support system. As a result, they each have access to a network of coemployees whom they may contact whenever they need assistance or direction.

For instance, HP's maternity support group offers a platform for young moms or "mothers to be" to seek counsel or assistance, which has been essential in easing their parenthood journey. Finally, organisations must put a priority on supporting women's growth since doing so will increase their commitment to and loyalty to the organisation.

Inclusion is a potent catalyst for corporate expansion. Before we can genuinely claim that inclusion has become the norm in our professional settings and beyond, there is still a long way to go. Adopting inclusion as a organisation objective is another of the main obstacles to establishing an inclusive workplace. Progress on inclusiveness must have the leadership's full support if it is to be sustained. Adoption of inclusion might run into problems when it becomes HR, the Women's Leaders Forum, or the Diversity Leader's "also" duty. Beyond the fact that employees are unaware of the policies, it also hinders promoting inclusion when the senior most leadership is not in charge of the policies.

Resistance to change is another obstacle to promoting inclusion inside organisations. Diversity and inclusion go far beyond just implementing best practises in the workplace; they also, to a large part, include educating people about correct conduct and developing a mindset that actively supports flexible work arrangements. These divisions are all equally vital and all demand similar efforts to be successful. To sum it all up, though, inclusiveness must become a priority for leaders and a corporate objective if it is to succeed.

A universal challenge is finding and keeping diverse talent. Here are six instances where taking action might strengthen a organisation's DIBE initiatives. Diversity is the term used to describe a group's distinctions in terms of age, aptitude, gender, colour, religion, and sexual orientation. The degree to which everyone feels valued, supported, and accepted at work, regardless of their background, is frequently described as inclusion. A supportive environment must be created for someone to be their truest and best self at work. Innovation has endless potential when a diverse and inclusive team works together. For many sectors, diversity at the top level is also a problem. This presents a problem in men-dominated fields like engineering and construction, for instance. For organisations throughout the world, finding and keeping a broad pool of talent is a constant problem. In order to give everyone the feeling that they can be themselves and do their best work, it is crucial to foster an inclusive culture. This fosters a sense of purpose and creates a welcoming atmosphere to retain the best employees.

Promoting inclusion throughout the organisation begins at the top. The goal and actual steps that collectively produce an inclusive atmosphere must be clearly stated by leaders. For instance, making investments in leadership development, implementing zero-tolerance and equitable employment rules, and connecting diversity and inclusion to organisation objectives. However, this isn't simply being driven by leadership. Everything we do has DIBE layers over it, and everyone contributes significantly to determining the culture of the business. We support a

"Respect for All" culture, which encourages our associates to treat everyone with respect. This is an extension of our "TakeCare" culture, in which we urge our employees to take excellent care of themselves. It involves proactively embracing a variety of strengths that a candidate may provide.

When it comes to hiring new employees, we make sure that everyone has an equal chance at success, regardless of their ethnicity, gender, sexual orientation, or any other characteristics covered by the law. Additionally, we put a lot of effort into internally celebrating and effectively conveying the ideals of inclusion at all levels of the organisation.

Globalization, technology, and demographic shifts open up new growth prospects for businesses while upending established organisational and commercial paradigms. People with various backgrounds contribute a variety in terms of knowledge, viewpoints, and attitudes. Organisations with greater diversity have access to a wider range of talent, increasing their capacity to compete. Due to informational diversity, these teams are also better equipped to target and distinctively service a variety of client markets, such as women, ethnic minorities, and LGBTQ+ groups, which control a rising amount of consumer income. Improved loyalty, cooperation, and employee satisfaction are all benefits of DIBE management. High achievers may be drawn to the surroundings as a result. Boost a organisation's reputation globally: Companies with improved DIBE have improved reputations with their clients, the supplier chain, the local communities, and the general public.

Many businesses have benefited from using remote and hybrid work methods to build inclusive, egalitarian, and diverse workplaces. The advantages that followed include improved internal efficiency and access to larger talent pools. Worldwide organisations made an abrupt shift to remote labour as a result of the rapid coronavirus epidemic. Organisations were uneasy about the transition to 100% remote work arrangements, which led to doubts about, among other things, employee productivity, engagement, and inclusion. Employees have a choice in where they work, especially elite talent. Many people take other factors into account in addition to the job, title, pay, and work policy. They ponder how a potential employer would respond to seeing the name of the organisation on their résumé. By using a hybrid work style, your organisation displays that it is progressive and aware of general demographic trends.

However, remote work eliminates the commuting time and time spent away from home, making it simpler for people to juggle work and family obligations. The urge to work remotely is high among women (68%), even after the epidemic has passed. Organisations may hire a wide range of people because of remote employment. Without employees, businesses cannot develop and run. On-site work is strongly opposed by the modern workforce. According to a Webex study, 57% of employees would think about quitting their employer if they had to spend more time in the office.

"The one true service we can do as an organisation and as a member of the leadership team to bring in, sustain, and most importantly, help an often lesser understood construct of diversity and inclusion thrive is by supporting any aspect, no matter how big or small."

The actions of leaders matter. In companies, senior executives set the agenda and communicate what is crucial.

Assuring that this is consistent with our mission, values, and organisational goals, while also improving the individual's sense of belonging on a daily basis To get a pulse on how our employees are feeling about their managers, teams, and the range of procedures and interactions that happen at key milestones in addition to their regular interactions, leadership backing and engagement are crucial.

Nowadays, talent development and upskilling are essential to every organisation's success. It provides a way for everyone to advance professionally, which in turn helps an organisation expand. The majority of businesses also create training and development programmes for their employee using data-driven insights. Training in motivational, product-related, and soft skills guarantees that the workforce's skills are improved. It is essential for raising professional satisfaction.

As a result, in order to transform a disengaged workforce into an engaged one, we must begin to view the inclusion of women as the rule rather than a societal favour. This supports businesses in achieving a more natural, balanced, and healthy style of working. According to a Yello poll, 83% of participants said that a better workforce balance would affect whether they accepted or rejected a job offer. This is a significant increase from the 64% of respondents who said the same thing five years ago. The value of inclusion and diversity in the workplace Although we may be familiar with these phrases and find them to be relevant, it's probable that we are unaware of the breadth of the topic at hand. A varied mix of women can include ladies from various cultures, ethnicities, languages, and colour spectrums, but it doesn't stop there.

How businesses are using remote employment to foster a diverse, egalitarian, and inclusive workplace?

Inclusion results from giving them an equal chance, listening to them, giving them an equal amount of assistance, and making them feel that their needs are being addressed. Focusing on the sense of belonging in the culture as managers and leaders benefits the business while also enabling you to reach your full leadership potential. Before the introduction of remote work, an organisation's employee was centred on the area surrounding its headquarters. Due to this lack of diversity in the local talent pool, recruiters had trouble finding applicants from underrepresented groups. With the advent of remote work, organisations can now hire and retain employees without having to worry about location prejudice or relocation expenses. The availability of remote work choices enables recruiters to hire and retain individuals from a variety of racial, geographic, and cultural backgrounds. This will inevitably help improve the organisational culture as well.

Organisations should focus on regular contact with the workforce and be more open and transparent, especially in hybrid situations. Organisations must create a workplace culture where employees enjoy collaborating and contribute to the organisation's success. How can leaders tackle discussions that question the meritocracy of recruiting people of colour? What strategy have you used? When there is a varied collection of individuals working, organisations across sectors have noticed improvements in decision-making, problem-solving, creativity, innovation, etc. This suggests that inclusion actually refers to selection based on merit. Inclusion has actually flourished along a path where each chance is merit-based.

By hiring from the largest pool of candidates across all categories, using the newest technology to upskill employee, and giving them a chance to shine, leaders can create an inclusive meritocracy. Naturally, we must also combat unconscious prejudice. Leaders may approach the meritocracy of diversity recruiting in a number of ways, including by inspiring their workforce, cultivating an empathic attitude, and promoting a listening culture.

What are some of the main changes in DIBE that organisations need to be ready for in the modern workplace?

The previous two years have seen a lot of change in workplaces, but more significantly, they have brought back to light the structural issues that underrepresented employees confront in our society and the consequences that can result from these issues if they are not addressed. Examining tech-enabled DIBE solutions will be one of the most significant changes. To support excellent DIBE results, leaders should use the potential of technologically enhanced solutions. Another change will be in how talent from all backgrounds is sought for and hired, enabling a varied workplace and fostering productivity via the fusion of many ideas. Additionally, it's important to enable equitable opportunities for everyone in order to build a diverse and inclusive ecosystem that is sustainable. The future of DIBE programmes will place more focus on hiring and giving women opportunities for professional advancement.

Today's business success is a result of cross-cultural collaboration to create novel goods. It is critical to stress that a diversity and inclusion programme is not about one person succeeding at the expense of others, but rather about fostering an inclusive environment where everyone is valued. A crucial first step is establishing a framework to foster diversity and inclusion. But in order to integrate diversity and inclusion into organisation culture, everyone must act in support of it. We still have a long way to go, like many of our colleagues, but we are on the path. Like many businesses, we started our multi-year strategy and programme for diversity and inclusion with gender, but we always strive to broaden it across every group we can. Research from both inside and outside the organisation now backs a strategy that goes beyond gender diversity.

Any type of discrimination in the workplace is unacceptable, including that based on gender, caste, handicap, age, ethnicity, means of support, marital status, etc. To prevent bias in any form, clear and well-defined policies must be established. In order to promote diversity inside organisations, HR directors must take the initiative. Companies should progressively take steps to introduce genuine mentorship for potential candidates, whether men or women, in order to support their professional success.

Diversity and inclusion are distinctly different, although frequently coupled. In a diverse organisation, a lack of inclusiveness might alienate a portion of the workforce. Working with a global workforce, for instance, entails interacting with individuals who speak various languages. Speaking a local language and assuming that their colleagues understand the situation might keep them from participating in the discussion. Everyone would feel more inclusive if the organisation practised communicating in a similar language. Practices for inclusiveness should be made clear to the entire organisation. The organisation's inclusion goals may benefit from regular feedback that captures employees' experiences inside the team or organisation. Organisations should value everyone's input and offer channels for ongoing feedback sharing in order to be inclusive.

To sum up, embracing diversity is a key to the success of any organisation, no matter how big or small, because it encourages a variety of thought patterns, introduces new ideas, and allows for the resuscitation of organisations, which is crucial during pandemics; as an organisation, you gain knowledge of other industries through the work experience of new hires; experience and agility are combined in multigenerational workforces; and these procedures may assist you in managing your stakeholders and clients while also fostering a feeling of community. If DIBE is implemented correctly, it may provide all of the solutions.

Having responsibility is one of the most crucial things you can do to ensure the success of a diversity and inclusion programme. You must establish goals, track your development, and hold others responsible. You should hold employees accountable for achieving diversity goals if you think diversity pays, which you should; it improves financial results like stock prices, return on assets, sales, and revenue. Microsoft also intends to link executive incentives to the success of the business's diversity initiatives. But how can you gauge achievement? One clear method is the diversity of new personnel. In truth, 65% of multinational corporations claim to have initiatives in place to broaden the diversity of their applicant pools. Another excellent indicator of the effectiveness of diversity and inclusion programmes is turnover. Everywhere in the globe, especially in relation to employee experience, DIBEs are a topic of discussion.

It's crucial to uphold the ideal of inclusiveness as we introduce diversity into the workplace. What one employee requires to feel included may differ from what another employee requires. People from different backgrounds may feel less valued in an organisation without inclusion, which might prevent them from achieving their full potential. As a result, we must make sure that every employee is treated with respect and heard if we want the organisation to succeed. Every organisation should make an effort to keep its productive employees. It's obvious that your organisation wouldn't want to fire its rock stars because hiring is often highly expensive for an organisation. We become receptive to each employee's individuality and find methods to recognise it when we choose diversity and inclusion approaches to improve the workplace. As a result, employees remain on the job longer since their differences are openly welcomed.

When inclusion becomes a "also" obligation for the HR, Women's Forum, or Diversity Leader, it might be difficult to implement. A truly inclusive organisation will stand out because inclusion will not only be an HR or DIBE leader's objective but a business agenda.

How do organisations go about incorporating allyship, inclusivity, and empathy into the work flow while dealing with a multigenerational workforce working in a hybrid environment? It takes time to become inclusive. It is a deliberate inclusion. And when mainstreaming it, it has to be an ongoing process that attempts to incorporate inclusiveness and allyship into the organisation's core values.

How can organisations avoid tokenism in their hiring practises and efforts to change their culture?

Accepting tokenism at face value is frequently the beginning of a self-inflicted trap. You can alter your recruiting practises to appear more inclusive, but diversity will only cause problems for your organisation's culture unless you genuinely embrace inclusion. A truly inclusive organisation will stand out because inclusion will be a business priority rather than merely the concern of HR or DIBE leaders. It will cease to be mere symbolism the day that you, as a leader, make it your agenda, the agenda of a business leader, making it clear and unwavering like all other organisation objectives.

"Though leading change may seem difficult, leaders and professionals must continually consider how they may make a positive difference in a strategic, long-lasting, and significant way. Having corporate purpose integrated into your organisation's business model may just be the first step toward running an all-encompassing organisation, but inclusive hiring and recruiting is a promising first step."

Humans have a fundamental desire for belonging, and we have modified our actions to attempt to decrease that urge, much like how we strive to prevent physical discomfort. Additionally, studies suggest that fostering a more inclusive workplace generates a greater sense of belonging, which in turn improves engagement and productivity. Regardless of their interest in the debate, people can develop empathy by focusing on a sense of belonging. Each of us may recall an occasion when we didn't feel like we belonged. We hope that sharing this common experience will lead to a better understanding of people from marginalised groups.

It is impossible to overstate the value of inclusion, fairness, and diversity in the workplace. However, when underdeveloped and half-baked tactics are put into practise, they frequently cause more harm than good, causing the same constituencies they are meant to help to completely disregard DIBE. Although there has been a noticeable change in attitudes, practical progress towards creating more inclusive workplaces has been agonisingly slow and, in some circumstances, has come to a complete standstill. There have been countless instances of inequality, diversity, and intolerance throughout human history. These vices have harmed humanity in a variety of ways. Unfortunately, it appears that we still have much to learn since these problems continue to plague our society.

More companies have made the journey to an inclusive, well-oriented workplace culture during the past ten years. It is essential to improving business growth and employee retention for the majority of enterprises. As a result, there is a greater emphasis on creating the ideal workplace rules and conditions to support a diverse workforce. The first step in supporting development, growth, and advancement for the organisation as well as for society at large is to ensure inclusivity. Considering DIBE (Diversity, Inclusion, Belonging, and Equality) from a Global Perspective Everywhere in the globe, especially in relation to employee experience, DIBEs are a topic of discussion.

How can we create a productive hybrid work environment?

We are all aware that much effort is being made to reimagine employment in the future. We still don't know the answers to so many crucial issues, including: what will cooperation look like? It's crucial to continuously ask, "Where does diversity, inclusion, and belonging (DIBEs) fit in?" throughout the entire job. Working with hundreds of groups over the past year has shown us that there has never been a stronger worldwide push for action on DIBEs. We have the chance to incorporate DIBs into the framework of how we create workplaces of the future, placing people at the centre, inspired by some of the events that occurred in the U.S. that have spread around the world and compelled businesses to participate in the discourse.

Consider the Asia-Pacific (APAC) area as an illustration. Geographically, racially, and culturally diverse as it is, there are variations in the DIBs debates here by nation that we need to take into account. However, some themes recur throughout the region and match the DIBs problems we observe globally.

In India, just 3% of CEOs and managing directors of organisations registered on the National Stock Exchange in 2019 were female. In Japan, women make 23.5% less money than men do. Women make up only 18% of CEOs in Australia.

Research demonstrates a vacuum in initiatives targeted at ethnic minorities and LGBTQ groups, indicating that DIBEs debates in the region that go beyond gender are still in their infancy. In many Asian countries, colorism is pervasive and has negative effects on inclusion both within and outside of the workplace. If we take gender as an example, we can see that development is sluggish and that there is still work to be done to increase representation and equity at all levels.

Only 34 lakh of the 1.3 crore people with disabilities in the workforce in India are now working. The daily drive to work is a problem that many of these folks frequently face. Even if these impairments may not impede their ability to do their jobs, what may appear to be a simple journey for individuals with normal mobility issues owing to physical, visual, or immune inadequacies can prove to be a significant difficulty. Organisations provide work for people with impairments by providing remote work opportunities. Internally, share tales and activities that foster diversity and inclusion while intentionally projecting a broader range of images and narratives. Include a formal commitment to promoting an atmosphere of diversity, inclusiveness, and personal growth, as well as human decency and respect, in the business conduct guidelines.

"In almost every profession worldwide, whether it be as a CEO or software engineer, the majority of women are still underutilised in terms of potential and leadership. Despite the fact that women make up roughly half (49.6%) of the world's population, this inequality still exists. "

Nevertheless, despite all these advancements, diversity and inclusion still face significant obstacles to overcome and goals to achieve. Businesses all over the world are continually working to improve the diversity and inclusion of all individuals as well as provide equal opportunity. Businesses all over the world are continually working to improve the diversity and inclusion of all individuals as well as provide equal employment opportunities for everyone.

Determine the reality of your existing position on DIBE. Raising awareness of the benefits of DIBE for attaining a competitive edge. Accept DIBE to increase and sustain talent acquisition and retention; recognise the benefits of an internal culture that inspires and involves everyone; and ensure that DIBEs are deeply ingrained and assimilated into your organisation's ethos.

"In order to transform a disengaged workforce into an engaged one, we must start to view the inclusion of women as the norm rather than a social favour. This supports businesses in achieving a more natural, balanced, and healthy style of working."
- Dr. Amit Das

References

- *Diversity and Inclusion Matters: Tactics and Tools to Inspire Equity and Game-Changing Performance, by Jason Thompson, Apr 2022.*
- *Belonging: The Key to Transforming and Maintaining Diversity, Inclusion and Equality at Work Paperback – Import, 12 May 2022 by Sue Unerman (Author), Kathryn Jacob (Author), Mark Edwards (Author).*
- *Diversity Equity and Inclusion Strategies for Facilitating Conversations on Race 2015 Edition by Caprice Hollins, Ilsa Govan , Rowman & Littlefield, Caprice Hollins, Ilsa Govan.*
- *Unconscious Bias + Diversity And Inclusion In Organizations + Equality & Equity (Diversity, Inclusion and Unconscious Bias Book 5) Kindle Edition by David George (Author) Format: Kindle Edition.*
- *Management and Diversity: Thematic Approaches (International Perspectives on Equality, Diversity and Inclusion Book 4) Kindle Edition by Jean-Francois Chanlat (Editor), Mustafa Özbilgin (Editor) Format: Kindle Edition.*
- *HR Rising!!: From Ownership to Leadership by Steve Browne*
- *Belonging at Work: Everyday Actions You Can Take to Cultivate an Inclusive Organization by Rhodes Perry, MPA*
- *People Processes: How Your People Can Be Your Organization's Competitive Advantage Hardcover – Import, 11 September 2018 by Rhamy Alejeal.*
- *The Fearless Organization: Creating Psychological Safety in the Workplace for Learning, Innovation, and Growth by*

Amy C. Edmondson

- *Strategic Human Resource Management: An HR Professional's Toolkit by Karen Beaven*
- *The Resource Management and Capacity Planning Handbook, A Guide to Maximizing the Value of Your Limited People Resources by Jerry Manas, 2014*
- *HR from the Outside In: Six Competencies for the Future of Human Resources by Dave Ulrich, Jon Younger, Wayne Brockbank, Mike Ulrich, 2011*
- *HR Transformation: Building Human Resources From the Outside In by Dave Ulrich, Wayne Brockbank, Jon Younger, Mark Nyman, Justin Allen , August 2009*
- *The Diversity Playbook: Transforming Business with Inclusion and Innovation Kindle Edition by Hephzi Pemberton (Author) Format: Kindle Edition.*
- *Diversity and Inclusion in Environmentalism (Routledge Studies in Environmental Justice) Paperback – Import, 3 June 2021 by Karen Bell (Editor).*
- *Performance through Diversity and Inclusion: Leveraging Organizational Practices for Equity and Results Hardcover – Import, 30 September 2021*
- *by Ruth Bernstein (Author), Paul Salipante (Author), Judith Weisinger (Author).*
- *The Definitive Guide to Sustainability & Diversity, Equity, and Inclusion: The Most Effective Way to Business Competitiveness Kindle Edition by Aurora Grion (Author), Giulia Pernisi (Author), Priyanka Banerjee (Author).*
- *Diversity & Inclusion: Why is Diversity and Inclusion so Important in the Workplace (Leveling Up 101) Kindle Edition by Euvouria LLC (Author) Format: Kindle Edition.*
- *Equity, Equality, and Empathy: What Principals Can Do for the Well-Being of the Learning Community Paperback – Import, 14 September 2022 by Richard D. Sorenson*

(Author).

- *Inclusion: Diversity, The New Workplace & The Will To Change Hardcover – Import, 1 June 2017 by Jennifer Brown (Author).*
- *Human Resource Management By Gary Dessler, Biju Varrkey, December 2017*
- *Talent, Transformation, and the Triple Bottom Line, How Companies Can Leverage Human Resources to Achieve Sustainable Growth by Andrew W. Savitz, Karl Weber, Edward E. Lawler, 2013*
- *Human Resource Management by Raymond Noe, John Hollenbeck, Barry Gerhart, Patrick Wright, 2020*
- *Human Resource Management, People, Data, and Analytics by Talya Bauer, Berrin Erdogan, David E. Caughlin, Donald M. Truxillo, 2019*
- *Equality & Equity: Today's Situation Of Equality In USA, UK And Other Multicultural Countries (Diversity, Inclusion and Unconscious Bias Book 4) Kindle Edition by David F. George (Author), 14 July 2021.*
- *Handbook of Research Methods in Diversity Management, Equality and Inclusion at Work Hardcover – Import, 31 August 2018 by Lize A.E. Booysen (Editor), Regine Bendl (Editor), Judith K. Pringle (Editor).*
- *Building Workplace Equality: Ethics, Diversity and Inclusion Paperback – Import, 1 August 2002 by Nelarine Cornelius (Author).*
- *Equality, Diversity & Inclusion: The Practical Guide: The essential handbook for terminology and communicating inclusion with dignity. Kindle Edition by Tony Malone (Author) Format: Kindle Edition.*
- *Lead the Change - The Competitive Advantage of Gender Diversity and Inclusion: The Competitive Advantage of Gender Diversity & Inclusion Paperback – Import, 31 May*

2020 by Kelly L Cooper (Author).

- *Bias Interrupted: Creating Inclusion for Real and for Good Hardcover – 16 November 2021 by Joan C. Williams (Author).*
- *Demystifying Diversity: A Handbook to Navigate Equality, Diversity and Inclusion Kindle Edition by Jiten Patel (Author), Gamiel Yafai (Author) Format: Kindle Edition.*
- *HBR's 10 Must Reads on Diversity (with bonus article "Making Differences Matter: A New Paradigm for Managing Diversity" By David A. Thomas and Robin J. Ely) Paperback – 30 June 2019 by Harvard Business Review (Author), David A. Thomas (Author), Robin J. Ely (Author), Sylvia Ann Hewlett (Author), Joan C. Williams (Author).*
- *Workplace Diversity & Inclusion + Proven Steps To Inclusive Leadership + Innate Biases (Workplace Diversity And Inclusion Book 4) Kindle Edition by Jennifer McKay (Author) Format: Kindle Edition.*
- *Innate Biases: How To Identify And Overcome Your Unconscious Prejudice (Workplace Diversity And Inclusion Book 3) Kindle Edition by Jennifer McKay (Author) Format: Kindle Edition.*
- *DEI Deconstructed: Your No-Nonsense Guide to Doing the Work and Doing It Right Hardcover – Import, 25 October 2022 by Lily Zheng (Author).*
- *Promoting Diversity, Equity, and Inclusion for Women After the COVID-19 Pandemic Paperback – Import, 30 June 2022 by Siham El-Kafafi (Editor).*
- *Organizing Inclusion: Moving Diversity from Demographics to Communication Processes (Routledge Studies in Communication, Organization, and Organizing) Hardcover – 12 May 2020 by Marya L. Doerfel (Editor), Jennifer L. Gibbs (Editor).*

- *Inclusive Leadership: The Definitive Guide to Developing and Executing an Impactful Diversity and Inclusion Strategy: - Locally and Globally Paperback – 25 October 2016 by Charlotte Sweeney (Author), Fleur Bothwick (Author).*
- *Cultures of Belonging: Building Inclusive Organizations that Last Kindle Edition by Alida Miranda-Wolff (Author) Format: Kindle Edition.*
- *Diversity within Diversity Management: Types of Diversity in Organizations: 22 (Advanced Series in Management) Hardcover – Import, 7 May 2019 by Dr Andri Georgiadou (Editor), Maria Alejandra Gonzalez-Perez (Editor), Miguel R. Olivas-Luján (Editor).*
- *Closing The Gap: 5 steps to creating an Inclusive Culture Paperback – Import, 10 March 2019 by Teresa Boughey (Author).*
- *Let Them See You: The Guide for Leveraging Your Diversity at Work Hardcover – 15 January 2019 by Porter Braswell (Author).*
- *Underestimated: A CEO's Unlikely Path to Success Paperback – Import, 11 October 2022 by Donald Thompson (Author).*
- *Inclusive Growth: Future-proof your business by creating a diverse workplace Paperback – Import, 28 January 2020 by Toby Mildon (Author).*
- *Neuro Diverse Workplace: An Employer's Guide to Managing and Working with Neurodivergent Employees, Clients and Customers Paperback – 19 December 2019 by Victoria Honeybourne (Author).*
- *Leadership in Diversity and Inclusion: Ultimate Management Guide to Challenging Bias, Creating Organizational Change and Building an Effective Diversity & Inclusion Strategy Kindle Edition by Eleanor Bowes*

(Author) Format: Kindle Edition.

- *The Diversity & Inclusion Glossary: A reference guide to key words that celebrate diversity and reduce inequalities. Kindle Edition by Tony Malone (Author), Sue Sanders (Foreword).*
- *The Importance of Diversity and Inclusion in the Workplace: From the Perspective of a POC (Person of Color) Kindle Edition by Camille Brewster (Author) Format: Kindle Edition.*
- *Managing Diversity and Inclusion: An International Perspective 2nd Edition, Kindle Edition by Jawad Syed (Author), Mustafa Ozbilgin (Author).*
- *Gender Diversity and Non-Binary Inclusion in the Workplace: The Essential Guide for Employers Kindle Edition by Sarah Gibson (Author), J. Fernandez (Author) Format: Kindle Edition.*
- *Male Perspectives on The Value of Women at Work Paperback – Import, 20 April 2021 by Susan Popoola (Author).*
- *Getting to Diversity: What Works and What Doesn't Kindle Edition*
- *by Frank Dobbin (Author), Alexandra Kalev (Author) Format: Kindle Edition.*
- *Diversity, Inc.: The Failed Promise of a Billion-Dollar Business Kindle Edition by Pamela Newkirk (Author) Format: Kindle Edition.*
- *Highly Effective Inclusion: Women in Workplace: The Potential They Bring Kindle Edition by Rachel Stephen (Author).*

About The Author

Dr. Amit Das, is a renowned executive advisor, consultant, educationist, author, speaker, counsellor, and coach whose 25+ years of business experience provides high-impact, practical solutions that support his clients' leadership development and organisational transformations. He worked for fortune 500 comapnies and left rich leagacy of organising transformational learning workshops. He has transformed more than 5000+ working executives through his path breaking capability building learning workshops. Dr. Amit Das is recognised as an innovative, principled thought leader who combines intellectual rigor and discipline with an ability to translate theory into practice. His operational skills are coupled with a strategic ability to analyse, develop, and implement successful strategies for profitability, growth, and sustainability.

Dr. Amit Das has a successful track record in aligning learning and training solutions to key business strategy with a strong focus on flawless execution excellence to facilitate individual, business divisional, and organisational performance. He keeps relentless focus on measuring training impact and ROI, people capability building graphs, training process governance, performance coaching, and strategic thinking. These have been some of his key individual success traits. His core capabilities include performance coaching, designing training and development frameworks, psychometric assessment and analysis, competency framework development and assessments, content design and facilitation of soft skills and leadership programmes, Learning Management Systems, Learning Impact Measurement, Talent Analysis, and Performance Coaching and Counselling.

Dr. Amit Das has authored multiple management and self-development books, like Redefining HRM, Create Your Leadership Edge, Love-Laugh- Live With Happiness, SMART Parenting @ Zero Cost, Building Organisational Capability, Ethical Road Map, Attomic Attention, BYPB, Redefining The Power Of Mentoring, Making The Most Future Fit Organisation, Redefining Talent Management, Defining Your Success Factors, Lead or Plead, Make The Most Of Your Life, Better Half or Bitter Half, Psychology Of Learning And Development, The Transformative Mind & Soul are few of them.

He has a Ph.D. and a Fellowship in strategic learning, along with his first class degrees in Human Resource Management, Marketing Management, International Business, and Corporate Laws from the top business schools in India. He is a certified Psychometric analyst, HR Analyst, OD Interventionist, Human Psychologist, Lifecoach, Leadership Developer, Black Belt (LSS), Strategic Thinker, Talent Analyst, certified professional trainer from the U.K. and certified behavioral coach from the U.S.A.

Dr. Amit Das likes googling, reading books, writing articles & books, cooking, listening to old melodies, and counselling people to unleash their true potential to build a strong nation. He is married and blessed with a son. He would love to hear about your experience after reading his books. You can email him and share your thoughts, or you can use his services for life coaching, positive behavioural counseling, educational support, and mentoring for young, promising students pursuing their B.B.A. and M.B.A. degrees.